THE ROAD TO
CEO

THE ROAD TO
CEO

The World's Leading
Executive Recruiters
Identify the Traits You Need
to Make It to the Top

SHARON VOROS

Adams Media Corporation
Avon, Massachusetts

Dedication

To my husband Andy, who has supported my authorial urges for more than twenty years; my children Sam and Meredith, whose humor and concern energized me; and my father, Ernest L. Voros, whose stories about FDR, Eugene Grace, and the Emperor Franz Josef prompted my fascination with leaders.

Published by
Adams Media Corporation
57 Littlefield Street, Avon, MA 02322. U.S.A.

ISBN: 1-58062-709-9 (paperback)

Printed in Canada.

J I H G F E D C B A

Library of Congress Cataloging-in-Publication Data
Voros, Sharon D.
The road to CEO : the world's leading executive recruiters identify the traits you need to make it to the top / by Sharon Voros.
p.   cm.
ISBN 1-58062-709-9 (paperback)
ISBN 1-58062-326-3 (hardcover)
1. Leadership. I. Title.
HD57.7 .V67   1999
658.4'092--dc21   99-028170

This book is available at quantity discounts for bulk purchases.
For information, call 1-800-872-5627.

Visit our exciting small business Web site at businesstown.com

CONTENTS

ACKNOWLEDGMENTS

The idea for *The Road to CEO: The World's Leading Executive Recruiters Identify the Traits You Need to Make It to the Top*, was inspired five years ago when my former colleague David B. Radden advised me that a resume alone does not an executive make. I first explored the concept of leadership presence in *The National Business Employment Weekly*, where my article prompted intense reaction and interest. Realizing I had hit a nerve, I vowed to pursue leadership presence further by finding out what America's top executive recruiters, who judge it on a daily basis, had to say about it.

This book would not have been possible without the contributions of the one hundred fifty executive search professionals, search industry experts, executive career consultants, and business gurus who shared their thoughts and experiences on what it takes to become an outstanding leader.

The insights, examples, and advice offered by these professionals filled hundreds of pages, enough to write an entire series of books on executive presence. We selected key comments and concepts from their input that best demonstrate the breadth and depth of thinking and action that executive presence prompts in the corporate world—across a variety of industries and national origins.

I am particularly grateful to the perspectives on the search business offered by industry gurus Chris Hunt and Scott Scanlon of Hunt-Scanlon Publishing, Joseph McCool of *Executive Recruiter News*, and Paul Hawkinson of *The Fordyce Letter*, who helped me develop, challenge, and advance my ideas. Their input was especially helpful in the early stages as I built the book's concept and fleshed out the key points to be addressed.

In addition to the executive recruiting community, I would also like to express my appreciation to Dr. John W. Boudreau and Dr. Renae Broderick of the Center for Advanced Human Resource Studies at Cornell University's School of Industrial and Labor Relations. In 1995, I began working closely with Cornell to research why executives change jobs. A salute as well to John Rau, CEO of Chicago Title Corporation and former dean of Indiana University's School of Business. Collaborating with John on *Secrets from the Search Firm Files* awakened a dormant desire to write a book of my own.

Kelly Mooney provided exceptional research support for the executive profiles and final list of executives who have leadership presence. Joan Scott's editorial suggestions were a big help in developing the book. And Jodi Holden's enthusiasm and encouragement helped me move through the slow spots.

Thanks also to my agent Jeremy Solomon, who was convinced my idea was a worthy one, and to my editor, Jere Calmes, who provided thoughtful guidance throughout the process.

—SHARON VOROS
Fort Worth

FOREWORD

by
PHILIPPE DE BACKER
Partner, Bain & Co., and author of
Maximum Leadership

Management fads come and go. However, the importance of corporate leadership as a determining factor of success has never been doubted. What, exactly, makes an executive a leader? In an era of increasingly fierce business competition worldwide, few questions spark as much controversy and debate.

The contrasting windows of management consulting and executive search have allowed me to witness first-hand the characteristics that enable leaders to achieve long-lasting, bottom-line results. As a consultant with Bain & Co., I have been privileged to work with global leaders who are committed to achieving lasting value by attracting talent of all kinds, developing new products, improving market valuation, conceiving new ways of creating and delivering products and services, and outshining the competition. Before joining Bain & Co., I was a partner in a global executive recruiting firm, where I assessed candidates for top management positions at major international organizations.

Leadership, after all, is the ability to consistently deliver extraordinary results by making decisions about values and resources. It's also the capacity for setting a strategy—allocating scarce resources in a differentiated manner that leads to sustainable results. Perhaps the most important element of leadership is execution: ensuring that a company's tactics and everyday activities reflect its strategy.

One of the best ways of exploring leadership style is to learn how executives approach their job, position themselves, and view their role. There's nothing so revealing as a first hand explanation about people, decisions, programs, techniques, mistakes, and achievements. In conversations with more than 160 top global executives for my book, *Maximum Leadership*, I was fascinated to discover that the management approach a CEO chooses has little to do with his or her personality. Instead, it is based on what the company needs. In a situation where a new strategy is crucial to the organization's success, maximum leaders will adopt a strategic approach, positioning themselves as the company's top visionary. A human assets approach allows the CEO to manage for success through people policies. An expertise approach positions the CEO as the champion of a specific, proprietary expertise. The box approach involves launching a complex set of procedures and expected behaviors that lead to success; and the change agent approach requires the CEO to act as the catalyst of transformation.

Recognizing their company's strategic situation and the management approach of its top leader is a key step for someone who seeks a senior management position in their current company—or a similar opportunity at another organization. It's unlikely a "box" manager will make much career headway in a company led by a "strategic" CEO. But no matter what management approach an executive ultimately adopts, leadership presence is crucial. Knowing when to present a message, how to persuade other people, and which rules of corporate etiquette to apply are as vital to climbing the career ladder as understanding microeconomic theory or having a Ph.D. in computer science.

Appearance and *poise* are the most basic aspects of leadership presence. Leaders realize they are in the spotlight and nothing they do or say goes unnoticed. Besides adopting the "uniform" that accompanies his or her position, leaders are composed and relaxed in social interactions.

Another fundamental of executive presence is *focus*, or an ability to concentrate without distraction and to progress despite interruptions. Most executives are bombarded by a constant stream of phone calls, interruptions, problems, and people issues. Those who can propel their agenda forward while dealing with the inevitable sub-issues that arise have a unique talent.

Intellect is a critical intangible, but it's not simply a matter of IQ, SAT scores, or academic pedigree. In this information age, the ability to digest a huge amount of information and integrate it with previous data to establish an ever-evolving grounding in reality is key to a successful management career.

Executives with a gift for detangling the complex, building stories from raw facts and talking in an unpretentious, straightforward manner have perhaps the most important leadership presence factor of all—strong *communication skills*.

Perhaps the most elusive leadership presence factor, *charisma* is the ability to arouse interest and excitement and is directly related to an executive's self-confidence and interest in other people. In many cases, charisma is grounded in *passion*—an unwavering commitment to the job and the organization that fuels an executive's performance and energy. Finally, *culture fit*—the ability to recognize and act on an organization's basic rules of behavior—is basic to how an executive is perceived and respected.

It's virtually impossible for an executive to rise to the top without a strong dose of leadership presence. Thanks to the weakening of corporate hierarchies, ours is the age of the group. As a management consultant, I've seen numerous executives with superb technical expertise but underdeveloped leadership presence. No matter how brilliant they are, they eventually land in a job where they don't have to manage many people. Often, they leave the company or are forced out.

The good news is, leadership presence can be learned, increased, and enhanced. In *The Road to CEO: The World's Leading Executive Recruiters Identify the Traits You Need to Make It to the Top*, Sharon Voros and one hundred fifty top executive recruiters provide specific strategies and tactics for assessing your current leadership presence, pinpointing areas of strength and weakness, and nurturing the intangible factors that will propel your career trajectory.

1

WHY LEADERSHIP PRESENCE?

Leadership presence—the package of intangibles like passion, social poise, energy, communication skills, and appearance—is what ultimately leads to a senior executive position.

There's no shortage of advice on how to supercharge your career and propel yourself into the executive suite. Over the last ten years, psychologists, consultants, and academic researchers have published hundreds of treatises on the attitudes, behaviors, and capabilities that distinguish top executives. There are scores of instruction manuals on ascending the pyramid of success for managers eager to fast-track their careers. But most are based on a flawed assumption: ambitious executive wannabes can propel themselves to the top of their company through hard work, self-sacrifice, and a little emotional intelligence—not to mention the right suit of clothes.

In the vast majority of CEO search assignments, the candidates all possess a basic level of experience and skills. But in almost every case, the soft skills—the leadership presence factors—needed for the job are more important than the hard skills.

TRINA GORDON, PARTNER, BOYDEN

The reality is that the American Dream in a navy blue suit has gone the way of lifetime employment. Even if it ever was a reality, bootstrapping yourself to the top through hard work is a quaint tradition. Today, as unemployment reaches a historic low and corporations are scrambling for managers, most companies find it simpler and cheaper to recruit executives who have been trained at another company's expense. Whipsawed by shifting stock markets, overseas competition, and evolving technology, most of today's employers have increasingly abandoned their traditional—but costly—role of training and grooming future executives. Those companies that do, like General Electric and Procter & Gamble, are looted continually by executive recruiters and lose much of their top talent to companies in need of saviors. Says E. Pendleton James of Pendleton James & Associates Inc.: "GE is a farm team for us headhunters."

In the late 1960s, only 9 percent of new leaders came from outside, according to *Business Week*. Now, between 25 percent and 40 percent of the CEOs at the top 1,000 public companies were recruited from the outside, and that number is likely to grow. According to 1998 research by the International Association of Corporate and Professional Recruiters, more than 60 percent of vacancies at the executive level are filled with external candidates.

ADVANCING DIAGONALLY

The message for a majority of today's 14 million executives and managers is clear: rising to the top is now a game of advancing diagonally through different companies and industries. As Lou Gerstner, Bruce Harreld, and other top-level zigzaggers have shown, a detour to another industry may be the quickest route to the top of the corporate ladder.

In reality, the diagonal pathways to the corner office are now shaped by executive recruiters—headhunters—who offer their clients links to thousands of talented executives and a well-honed, discreet system for soliciting, screening, and hiring them. Although retained search fees can reach one-third of the new executive's annual compensation—not insignificant for an executive with a million dollar pay package—most large organizations find it well worth the expense to outsource the distasteful task of procuring talent from competitors. Like honeybees, recruiters today cross-pollinate the executive suites of most major companies, professional service firms, and venture-backed startups.

There's another reason recruiters have taken over the pathways to the executive suite: they provide institutionalized patience to the process of selecting a key executive. As companies seek to avoid the internal and external damage an executive like "Chainsaw" Al Dunlap, former CEO of Sunbeam, can wreak, they are ever more deliberate about selecting leaders and increasingly use executive recruiters to calm their boards and handle the heavy lifting of executive selection.

YOUR RESUME IS JUST THE START

Few executives with an eye on the corner office realize that a headhunter's recommendation is based on criteria that have little to do with accomplishments, career progression, resume power, or even snappy answers to interview questions. Professional accomplishments and content are only the beginning: leadership presence—the package of intangibles like passion, social poise, energy, communication skills, and appearance—ultimately land someone a senior executive position, no matter how good his or her credentials.

> *For senior positions, resumes are almost secondary. What's really critical is boardroom presence, and the ability to present ideas effectively and take ownership in making things happen.*
> DONALD C. CLARK, PARTNER,
> RAY & BERNDTSON

When I first began working with executive recruiters more than a dozen years ago, I was surprised to learn that a stellar career history and track record of success were necessary but insufficient requirements for a top management position. While standard "resume factors" like promotions, results, financial success, and P&L experience are important factors in rising to the top, most experienced recruiters are cynical about resumes, which can be custom-tailored to suit virtually any opportunity. They admit that leadership presence is almost always the determining factor in a client's decision to hire or reject a candidate. Says Jay Gaines, president of his own retained search firm, "On average, leadership presence and chemistry count for 70 percent of most hiring decisions. Performance and track record, only 30 percent." Agrees Rich Hardison, president of Hardison & Company, "The importance we place on leadership presence has changed dramatically since I entered the search business 25 years ago. Back then, performance, knowledge and skill were twice as important as presence. Today, presence is twice as important as performance and skills. We still have to find candidates with the right capability, but have to be far more conscious of the presence factor."

PLAYING THE GAME

Leadership presence is a critical requirement for a manager interested in advancing his or her career. If you seek a fast track to a top position, odds are you will move ahead every three to four years by changing companies, according to research by Cornell University's Center for Advanced Human Resource Studies. And it's likely you'll do so through a headhunter. In fact, you have almost certainly met with a recruiter, or talked to one on the phone, at least once in the past year.

While many of the opportunities recruiters dangle may not appeal to you, some certainly will. But if a headhunter is involved, you can be sure you're not the sole candidate for the job. You can dramatically improve your chances of landing the positions that interest you by knowing how headhunters evaluate executive presence.

In *The Road to CEO,* the world's top executive recruiters reveal the surprising realities of how management talent is judged and selected. *The Road to CEO* will show you:

- *How recruiters assess a candidate's executive presence. The Road to CEO* will help you master today's executive selection process and gain the job offers you really want. You'll discover how recruiters determine which leadership presence factors are critical, and which are expendable. You'll learn how recruiters pinpoint and assess whether or not you have "it," including the cues they look for, and understand how they communicate your leadership presence quotient to their client.

- *Where you stand on the leadership presence factor.* Chapter 5 provides an informal diagnostic test that can help you assess your leadership presence quotient and understand how you come across to the recruiters who can open doors or send you back to your current job.

- *Who has leadership presence.* You'll take an in-depth look at two executives with off-the-scale leadership presence quotients and read about hundreds of real-life examples that illustrate how presence—or lack thereof—can boost or deep-six a candidate's career plans. For the first time anywhere, you'll see recruiters' nominations for today's most presence-savvy executives.

- *How to enhance your leadership presence.* You'll gain firsthand advice from America's top headhunters on how to strengthen your presence, fortify weak areas and disguise problem spots, learn ten rules for aceing—or blowing—the interview, the primary testing ground of presence, and explore the fifteen questions that recruiters ask most. No surprise—what you know and what you've accomplished can have very little to do with how you are judged.

If you want to know how savvy executives drive their careers and what recruiters look for in executive candidates, if you want to move your career onto the fast track, then this book is for you. For the first time, *The Road to CEO* reveals the surprising reality of how executives become executives.

2

IT'S NOT
JUST WHAT
YOU'VE DONE

*No matter how good your business credentials and solid your
achievements, they're only the minimum requirement. Your
intangible qualities drive your success as a leader.*

A major executive search firm recently recruited a new
vice president of public affairs for a Fortune 1000 energy
company. On paper, the firm's top candidate had it all:
experience that matched the search specs, a good reputation among his peers, a law degree, Washington experience.
On the phone he was well spoken, dynamic, and compelling. But when he arrived for a personal interview with
the recruiter wearing a polyester suit and carrying a
Naugahyde briefcase, the recruiter moved him to the bottom of the list. Despite the candidate's superior accomplishments, it was clear to the recruiter that he wouldn't fit.
The candidate who got the job? An executive with a less-
than-perfect background who looked and acted the part.

In another case, a headhunter sought a new CEO for a major telecommunications company. One candidate's credentials were exceptional: five years as CEO for a large cellular company, promotions every two years, and a strong reputation for results in a highly competitive business. The candidate was interested in the position and excited about the long-term potential for his career. But a meeting with the recruiter at O'Hare Airport axed his chances for the job: the candidate couldn't sit still, called his office during the interview, and looked over the recruiter's shoulder continually, apparently concerned that someone from his company would see him talking to a headhunter. The executive who got the job? One who made the recruiter come to his home in the evening, away from the prying eyes of insiders and outsiders.

> *Companies may describe a next-generation executive, re-engineered for the new century. But more often than not, they are drawn to the candidate who has the same mix of qualities that has always added up to success in business. They want someone who is willing to work unbelievably hard, make personal sacrifices, communicate a powerful sense of mission, and stay focused on the issues and challenges that will determine the company's long term success.*
> WINDLE B. PRIEM, VICE CHAIRMAN AND COO, KORN/FERRY INTERNATIONAL

In a third case, a recruiter seeking an entry-level associate for a major management consulting firm pinpointed a candidate with ideal skills and potential from an Internet dredge. With an electrical engineering degree from MIT and three years of experience designing and installing computer systems for Fortune 50 companies, the candidate fit the consulting firm's ideal profile.

Although he had probably received three headhunter calls that day, he agreed to meet with the recruiter. But two hours into the interview, the recruiter excused herself: although Mr. Perfect looked great on paper, he couldn't keep his mouth shut. She knew his continual chatter would turn off her client. The person who got the job? A newly minted college graduate with social poise, well-honed communication skills, but less than ideal computer capabilities.

ACCOMPLISHMENTS ARE JUST THE BEGINNING

When I attended the Wharton School in the late 1970s, several classmates stood out as genuine "high-pots"—high potential MBA candidates who seemed destined for great things in life. There was the brilliant but acerbic student who helped the school's top finance professor invent a new investment management model; the bright but garrulous marketing major who had the last word in every classroom discussion; the hyper-motivated career monger who had himself videotaped weekly so he could perfect his interviewing skills. Although these "high-pots" left business school with top jobs—consulting positions with McKinsey & Company and corporate finance posts at brand-name investment banking houses—they now hold middle management positions or technical jobs where they focus on a small segment of business and are shielded from other people.

Like many who have served corporate America for twenty plus years, I have also crossed paths often with "steamrollers," executives with numerous notches on their belts and scalps in their wake. Typically hard-charging overachievers, these people gain regular promotions, bigger responsibilities, and fancier titles. But despite their bottom-line results, someone up above finally recognizes that the steamroller's subordinates and colleagues are complaining and leaving the company in a steady stream—and the ax falls.

And most of us know a few "low-pots" who barely graduated from college, usually because they spent four years partying. I've been continually amazed how many of these folks now hold senior management positions in some of the world's top companies. Most of these executives have few illusions about their intellectual skills and realize they ratcheted themselves up the corporate hierarchy by working well with people, acting the part with distinction, and playing the recruiting game with panache.

IT'S NOT JUST HOW SMART YOU ARE

These examples and a host of others underscore a simple reality of today's corporate world: No matter how good your business credentials and solid your achievements, they're only the minimum requirement for gaining an executive-level job. You can have a Harvard MBA, intellectual brilliance, and a history of successful projects. You can have the right job at the right time with the right boss. All of these "resume factors" will likely gain you access to a solid management position. But without leadership presence, you aren't likely to move up to a top job—in your current company or a new organization. In fact, you're likely to be stuck in your current job or even laid off. And it's true even in startup companies, fast growing computer software producers, and companies that eschew the corporate pyramid.

> *The higher you go in an organization, the more complete the package needs to be. The candidate's technical capability has to go unquestioned. Clients expect someone with education, experience, a record of success, as well as interpersonal skills and charisma. Lots of people are smart enough to be a CEO; what sets apart the candidates who deserve to be CEO is leadership presence.*
> CHUCK SWEET, PRESIDENT,
> A.T. KEARNEY EXECUTIVE SEARCH

Anyone who has watched an American presidential campaign knows that brainpower and accomplishments are merely the entry ticket for inclusion on the ballot. Energy, desire, looks, charm, and communication skills are essential to victory. So it is in business. But defining what it takes to be a business leader is not an easy task. Academic researchers like Warren Bennis, Jay Conger, and Daniel Goleman have spent their careers observing top executives in an attempt to identify the attitudes, behaviors, and capabilities that differentiate them from other human beings. Other consultants have attempted to pinpoint what distinguishes strong leaders from run-of-the-mill managers by surveying customers and employees. Their findings? A wide and often conflicting array of theories about executive thinking, childhood experiences, emotional intelligence, and even executive mysticism. And a few actionable tactics that an ambitious manager can start applying now to boost his or her shot at a leadership position.

GATEKEEPERS TO THE EXECUTIVE SUITE

A recruiter's job isn't merely a matter of sifting through resumes and picking the one that matches the job description. Says Gerard R. Roche, chairman of Heidrick & Struggles and perhaps the world's best-known executive recruiter, "Anybody can spot a top performer and compare a resume to a set of specs. The real art of search is scoping out the intangible qualities that will make a candidate win the job and succeed once they're there." "Executive presence is the soft underbelly of what makes a leader," agrees Dennis Carey, managing director of Spencer Stuart's Philadelphia practice.

> *A resume is a marketing document. It's our job to get beyond it and explore what the executive is really like and what he or she really did.*
> JOE ONSTOTT, MANAGING DIRECTOR,
> THE ONSTOTT GROUP

Recruiters like Roche, Carey, and Onstott have built their careers selecting and recommending executives, from controllers to vice presidents to CEOs of the world's major corporations. With half of all corporate executives now recruited to their organizations from the outside, headhunters have successfully channeled thousands of executives into the world's executive suites. Masters of seeing beyond the resume to the intangible factors that enable an executive to succeed or fail in a new situation, recruiters are critical gatekeepers to the doors of the executive suite. They play a key role in shaping the quality and effectiveness of a company's management team.

EXPLORING THE MYSTERIES
As vice president of communications for a large executive search firm conducting thousands of recruiting assignments

every year, I became fascinated with the communications that recruiters use to ply their trade. From the time I first entered the executive search profession in 1984, head-hunters regularly asked me to help them improve the style, format, and content of their "writeups," the six- to eight-page reports for clients that summarize a candidate's capabilities and suitability for a position. Over and over again I read a familiar litany: leadership presence—not revenues generated, growth achieved, market share won—was the critical factor in a candidate's suitability for a position. Like anyone trained as a reporter, I often found myself suggesting that the recruiters provide specific evidence of leadership presence. And once I began pushing my colleagues for more detail, I discovered a hoard of fascinating factors that recruiters say affect someone's ability to lead.

Leadership presence is an aura based on the individual's grooming, dress, handshake, communication style, energy, and charisma that shapes others' impressions. Presence involves much more than the physical—you don't have to be tall, dark, and handsome to have it. Confidence, energy level, and communications skills are also key.
JACQUES P. ANDRE, PARTNER, RAY & BERNDTSON

And so began the inquiry that has ultimately led to this book. To explore the mysteries of presence further and pinpoint what it takes over and above a stellar resume to win a top-level management position, I asked 160 of America's top executive recruiters how they define and judge a candidate's intangible attributes. My purpose: to uncover the not-so-obvious but oh-so-important criteria that can help ambitious managers move to the top and make the ones who are there more effective.

This effort has woven together several professional strands from my own career. As a journalist, I have used sourcing and research to explore facts, gather evidence and opinions, and weave a story. I've gone back to my professional roots as a market researcher to distill the opinions of recruiters regarding this elusive topic. And through my executive search background, I've become intimately acquainted with the recruiting process as well as many individual search assignments. I am also privileged to know most of the world's top recruiters, who enthusiastically provided me with extensive written and oral input on presence.

THE TOP RECRUITERS SPEAK

The experts we called on to dissect leadership presence were the executive recruiters cited in *The New Career Makers,* a directory of the top men and women employed in retainer-type executive search firms. The recruiters cited in the book stand in the top 2 to 3 percent of the 8,000 to 10,000 recruiters who practice headhunting today in corporate America. Selected by their peers as well as CEOs and top human resource executives at the largest public and private corporations, venture capital firms, professional, trade, and governmental organizations, these recruiters don't hunt heads for a bounty. They get paid whether or not they are successful in finding a willing candidate for the position, and are paid only by employers—not individuals seeking jobs. With generalist practices—few specialize in one industry group—the top recruiters focus primarily on finding executives whose annual compensation exceeds $150,000. Each recruiter conducts an average of twelve to fifteen search assignments every year.

Representing every U.S. geographic region, as well as Canada and Mexico, the recruiters provide a geographically diverse perspective. The group averages nearly twenty-three years of executive recruiting experience. Although the youngest is forty-one at this writing, many have continued to conduct search assignments well past standard retirement age. As recruiter John Sibbald, who compiled *The New Career Makers,* says, "Old headhunters never die; they just dial away."

We asked the recruiters to complete a two-page questionnaire about:

- why leadership presence is critical to a manager's career trajectory
- what elements, traits, factors, and behaviors comprise an executive's "presence"
- which of these factors is most critical in forming the individual's presence
- how they diagnose and assess executive presence
- who has presence
- if and how executives can enhance their presence

The recruiters responded in force: More than 125 returned completed questionnaires to us. To gather the case studies and stories to illustrate their perspectives and recommendations, we conducted in-depth interviews with selected respondents. We also supplemented their input through interviews with an additional twenty-five recruiters to explore executive presence in detail and pinpoint real-life cases in which it was a deciding factor for the recruiter or the client.

YOU KNOW IT WHEN YOU SEE IT

According to the top recruiters, leadership presence is probably the single most important factor in your ability to become a top executive. Paul McCartney, president of Technology Partners and one of the top headhunters in the high-tech industry, summarizes the general feeling of the top recruiters when he says, "Rarely will we meet with candidates for a CEO position unless they're fully qualified. We meet to assess leadership presence."

Like pornography, leadership presence is hard to define, but clients, customers, employees, and others "know it when they see it." Nobody can tell you how to measure it, but everybody is an armchair expert. Everyone has an opinion. And everyone is more than willing to dispense advice to anyone else who will listen.

Most recruiters agree that presence has basic elements, but it's also relative: the degree of confidence, energy, and other presence factors needed depends on the company's environment. When a manager has to interact extensively with other people, presence becomes a critical necessity. At higher levels of an organization, diplomacy and the ability to influence other people are critical as well. It's less critical lower in an organization.

First impressions are key. While an individual's grooming and dress shape how he or she is perceived, presence involves more than just the physical—you don't have to be tall, dark, and handsome to have it. Confidence, energy level, and communication skills are essential. Managers with presence assert themselves, offer a hand first, ask questions, and appear interested. In most cases, they speak without a significant regional accent. They are self-confident and gracious and can conduct a conversation with people at a variety of levels. They are usually blessed with the "gift of gab" and well read, using quotations from business leaders or other well-known people to introduce, reinforce, or conclude points. Typically gregarious, they seek out opportunities to be with customers, colleagues, and employees at all levels.

But presence involves more than cocktail party skills. Like private investigators, recruiters look for evidence on everything that doesn't show up on paper, from punctuality to abstract thinking skills. According to 160 top executive recruiters, presence is a package of eight key factors that can elevate an ordinary, successful manager from the land of cubicles to the boardroom:

Factor	% of recruiters indicating factor was extremely or very important in determining a candidate's executive presence
Focus	93.4
Intellect	89.5
Charisma	86.9
Communication skills	82.9
Passion	81.7
Culture fit	76.8
Poise	74.5
Appearance	68.1

Focus. Executives with presence are able to rivet their attention to an idea, person, or task at hand. Committed to the long term and the "big picture," they are rarely distracted from their own agenda by setbacks, interruptions, or fighting the fires that constitute a big part of any manager's daily routine.

Intellect. An executive's ability to see an issue, decision, or opportunity in a larger context and view it from many perspectives is a crucial factor in his or her executive presence. Executives with presence are usually quick studies who can digest complex theories, mountains of data, and tangled emotional situations and propose solutions easily.

Charisma. This refers mainly to an executive's emotional intelligence, his or her ability to demonstrate self-confidence, intensity, and commitment while appearing interested, caring, and concerned.

Communication skills. For recruiters—and for many of the boards that ultimately hire top executives—how executives say something is often more important than what they say. Executives with presence have a knack for simplifying the complex, reducing an intricate concept or maneuver to a one-page chart, and presenting an idea, issue, or directive with simplicity, humor, and sincerity.

Passion. There are no reluctant leaders: the most effective CEOs and senior level executives want a top level management job, and they want it badly. They demonstrate an extraordinarily high level of energy. Many recruiters say that the best managers are—or act as though they are—in love with their company.

Culture fit. Executives with presence are focused on more than just the bottom line: they have a keen sense of their organization's values, operational behaviors, and attitudes about change and recognize these factors as they move their agenda into place in the organization.

Poise. Executives with presence are socially adept. They are well schooled in basic social graces and maintain a relaxed composure in virtually all business situations.

Appearance. Senior executives are constantly on stage and must not only act the part, but look the part. In the United States, this means adopting the attire and grooming of the upper middle class.

LEADERSHIP PRESENCE—WHAT IT ISN'T

While recruiters are familiar with the concept of leadership presence, many of the business executives, journalists, and others I consulted in the course of writing this book were somewhat mystified by the term. Some thought it meant emotional intelligence, chemistry, management style, or even character. Some were curious how recruiters measured it given the limited time and access they often have to a candidate's job record and personal style. Others wondered how presence had value if there was no empirical basis for it or quantitative system to measure it.

The recruiters were very clear that leadership presence isn't simply one of the following:

Emotional intelligence, a concept introduced by Daniel Goleman in his landmark 1996 book of the same name, refers to people's capacity for recognizing their own feelings and those of others, motivating themselves, and managing emotions in themselves and in their relationships. According to Goleman, emotional intelligence is distinct but complementary to academic intelligence or cognitive capacities as measured by IQ. Many people who are book smart but lack emotional intelligence end up working for people who have lower IQs than they but who excel in emotional intelligence skills. A high level of emotional intelligence is just one very important aspect of executive presence.

Management style is the collection of tactics and behaviors leaders or managers employ to move their organizations toward success. Management style is dictated by the company's business situation, which includes marketplace dynamics, the company's competitive position, its human and technical capabilities, culture, cost structure, inheritance, and future. Many models of management style have been put forth since management became a discipline in the 1930s.

Management style can be, but is not necessarily, an extension of a manager's personality. In fact, many of the most successful leaders have adopted an approach that forces them to rise above their natural inclinations. Dana Mead, the soft-spoken, subdued CEO of Tenneco, had to adopt a fire-and-brimstone change agent leadership style to lead the $3 billion diversified company away from a highly politicized capital allocation system and a compensation program that rewarded meaningless goals. Abraham Lincoln—a man so modest and unassuming he wrote, "I do not think myself fit for the Presidency"—steered the United States through its greatest crisis.

Leadership presence transcends management style because it provides an executive with the essential credibility and strength needed to manage using a specific style.

Character, according to psychology textbooks, is the term for the motivational aspects of a person's mental life that supply energy or driving force for his or her behavior. These aspects can be inborn or acquired through experience. According to recruiting legend Russell Reynolds, character is the mechanism by which a person makes decisions and discriminates between right and wrong.

Selected aspects of someone's character—energy and passion, for example—are key components of presence. Character also influences other leadership presence factors such as communication skills, intellect, and poise. Character is unrelated to a fundamental executive presence variable: appearance.

Culture fit, or alignment between the executive's approach and "how we do things around here," is, like emotional intelligence, only one aspect of presence.

Chemistry refers to rapport with the organization's board of directors or the hiring manager. As many recruiters insist, companies don't hire executives, people hire them, and they are more likely to offer a job to candidates who reflect their own image and share similar viewpoints, management approaches, and experiences. Even executives with excellent people skills and emotional intelligence can fail to gain rapport with a key board or management committee member, particularly a picky or difficult one.

Chemistry is the wild card of executive recruiting. Usually the deciding factor in who gets the job offer, chemistry doesn't typically become an issue until the fundamental requirements—experience, accomplishments, and presence—are fulfilled. "Sometimes chemistry can be 95 percent at senior management level," says Rod Monahan, a recruiter with D. E. Foster Partners.

Each of the 160 recruiters who contributed to *The Road to CEO* had a distinctive set of of lessons to offer ambitious executives. But there's one thing they all agree on: success in a management position takes more than a first-class resume. The examples and case studies presented in this book underscore a simple reality of today's business world: today's leaders offer more than native smarts, specialized knowledge, and business fundamentals. And for the recruiters who increasingly serve as the gatekeepers of corporate America's executive suites, leadership presence is the touchstone for determining management potential.

This book summarizes their insights, perspectives, and "war stories."

3

MANAGING YOUR CAREER: THE NEW REALITIES

Even if they are happy with their current job, most executives stay plugged into the career market to keep abreast of opportunities.

Before downsizing and restructuring, corporations sought lifetime employees whose commitment to the company was paramount. In turn, executives trusted their employers to help them develop executive presence, boost their careers upward on a regular schedule, and protect their tenure. In 1965, the era of the Company Man, the average CEO had spent fifteen years with his organization. Like gemstones, executives were molded and shaped by their environments over time. Corporations promoted from within, drawing their entire management team from the cadres of executives they trained.

When I was growing up in Bethlehem, Pennsylvania, in the 1960s, the big company in town was Bethlehem

Steel, once a mighty international behemoth with 300,000 employees and manufacturing operations throughout the United States. Like most large corporations during that era, "The Steel" was committed to developing executives with presence. The company's exhaustive executive training program, "The Loop," shaped raw recruits hired directly from Ivy League schools and top state universities into polished executives with charisma, energy, focus, and all the other factors that constitute executive presence at The Steel. The recruits who survived eighteen months of basic classroom training and apprenticeships in various manufacturing operations emerged as consummate insiders who knew the organization's strengths and weaknesses, dressed like top executives, and walked, talked, and ate like top management.

For the few companies whose training programs failed to produce needed management talent, there was the old boy network—informal recruiting through college classmates, fraternity brothers, or social clubs.

THREE AND A HALF YEARS WITH EACH COMPANY

But neither internal promotion nor the old boy network could churn out enough candidates to fill the increasing number of management slots needed for expanding companies in the late 1960s. Rapid growth forced companies to poach executives from competitors, fueling the dramatic rise of the executive search business. "The average executive spends three to four years in a company nowadays," says Chip McCreary, CEO of Austin-McGregor International, a boutique search firm.

The re-engineering, downsizing, and industry consolidation of the late 1980s fundamentally changed how organizations plan for management succession and virtually eliminated the tradition of internal management training. With few exceptions, companies have abandoned the tradition of developing their own leadership talent. Even IBM and Coca-Cola—once the paradigms of executive training and development—now acquire a significant chunk of their executives on the open market.

YOU'RE ON YOUR OWN

As we enter the twenty-first century, corporate America provides a paradoxical set of demands to the manager with ambitions for top leadership positions. Companies want executives with superior resumes, long-term perspective, and leadership presence. At the same time, they are increasingly unwilling to provide the long-term training and development required to forge genuine presence. Companies now are inclined to buy it on the outside through the services of executive recruiters and, increasingly, through the Internet.

The bad news is executives now have to develop presence on their own. With the average executive changing companies more than six times during his or her career, high turnover in the executive ranks is a fact of life, and most managers realize that defensive career management is a necessity for economic survival.

WHO IS THE TYPICAL EXECUTIVE?

When I headed corporate communications and marketing for the executive search firm Ray & Berndtson, I conducted a series of opinion research studies on more than 1,800 executives with Cornell University's Center for Advanced

Human Resources. The purpose? To explore how senior executives were managing their careers. The sample represented a cross section of successful middle and senior managers in the United States, and the average respondent was a person employed at a company with more than $200 million in annual sales and more than 800 employees. With an annual compensation averaging $187,400, he held a position approximately two levels below the company's CEO and had been with the company an average of six years. The typical executive had eight promotions and it had been 3.3 years since his or her last promotion.

Despite a grueling work schedule that required them to spend an average of 4.5 nights per month away from home, 60 percent of the executives said they were satisfied with their current jobs. Much of their satisfaction may have stemmed from their company's success: the average annual growth rate of their organizations was 15 percent in each of the past three years, and the executives said their companies had been 63 percent successful in meeting their strategic goals. More than half of executives described the business environments for their companies as good.

Work is essential to the self-image of most executives. Nearly two-fifths of respondents said work was the most important aspect of their lives, followed closely by family. Leisure and religion were typically low-priority factors, as was community, reflecting the general drift of the upper middle classes away from volunteer and charitable organizations.

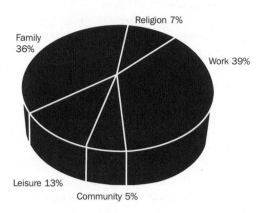

JOB STRESS

Today's executives are carrying a heavier emotional load.
Since the mid-1990s, stress levels among managers have
risen an average of 25 to 30 percent, and the 1,880 executives surveyed reported sixteen factors that cause quite a bit
or a great deal of stress:

Job Stress Factor	Executives who say factor causes quite a bit or a great deal of stress
Degree to which politics, not performance, affects organization's decisions	48%
The lack of job security I have	31%
Degree to which my career seems stalled	26%
Number of projects and assignments I have	26%
The amount of red tape I have to go through to get my job done	26%
Time pressures I experience	25%
Volume of work that must be accomplished in the allotted time	25%

Amount of time I spend on my work	22%
Amount of time I spend in meetings	22%
Conflicting demands of my position	22%
Ability to understand clearly what is expected from me on the job	16%
Number of phone calls and office visits I have during the day	15%
Opportunities for career development I have had	15%
Scope of responsibility my position entails	14%
Amount of responsibility I have	13%
Amount of traveling I must do	13%

HIGH ASPIRATIONS, DISAPPOINTING REALITY

Executives seek employment situations in organizations that provide the greatest career success. They believe that companies that are market-driven, innovative, outcome-oriented, and respectful provide a culture where they can flourish. However, many feel their current company's culture doesn't match up to the ideal on these attributes:

Percent of respondents indicating that attribute represents their:

	Ideal company	Current company
Market driven	73%	53%
Innovative	65	32
Outcome oriented	61	63
Respect for people	54	33
Team oriented	45	30
Aggressive	38	46
Continually changing	23	47
Stable	12	26
Detail oriented	7	40

Not surprisingly, the greater the difference between the ideal and current situations, the more likely they are to be dissatisfied and looking for a new job. In fact, the discrepancy between actual and ideal accounts for more than 60 percent of executive job satisfaction levels and intention to leave the current company.

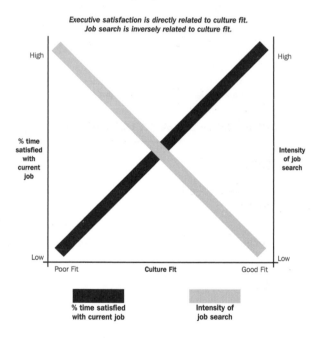

Executive satisfaction is directly related to culture fit.
Job search is inversely related to culture fit.

NO ONE DOESN'T TAKE A CALL

Since 1995, there's been a fundamental shift in how executives view their careers. It used to be difficult to pry an executive loose from a senior corporate position. Now, as many recruiters say, "No one doesn't take a recruiter's call." Why? Because they know it's the most expedient way to advance their career.

Our research found that:

Today's executives are working harder than they want to. As corporations contract and restructure, executives have fewer subordinates and are less able to delegate work. They spend more time in the office, and they're also carrying a heavier emotional load. Most managers work an average of fifty-seven hours per week, nine hours more than they desire. In contrast, they're spending less time than they'd like with their children and leisure activities.

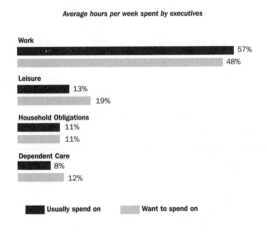

Average hours per week spent by executives

Work
57%
48%

Leisure
13%
19%

Household Obligations
11%
11%

Dependent Care
8%
12%

Usually spend on   Want to spend on

Executives are less committed to their present company, even though they are basically satisfied and are receiving raises and promotions. These executives were perceptive enough to realize that the old social contract—do good work and you'll get promoted—between U.S. companies and their executives had expired. Today, neither unconditional loyalty nor good work guarantees a job, let alone a promotion. Unable to count on their companies for permanent employment, nearly three in ten executives researched said they would leave their current position as soon as they found something better.

Companies can no longer rely solely on employee loyalty as a retention tool because there are fertile opportunities and incentives outside the company walls.
JEFFREY E. CHRISTIAN, PRESIDENT, CHRISTIAN & TIMBERS

Executives are moving into high gear to change jobs. Although most executives are relatively satisfied and say they have opportunities for promotion, they are exploring the job market more actively than they did five years ago. More than three-quarters of the 1,880 executives surveyed revised their resume, sent it to a prospective employer, or participated in a job interview with an executive recruiter or a hiring manager at another company. Most executives also spent several hours per week looking for new positions and contacted twenty-nine companies about possible job opportunities.

Top performers are highly marketable. Despite re-engineering and downsizing, companies are actively seeking management talent. Three-quarters of the executives in the Cornell research studies believed they had alternative employment possibilities. The executives surveyed say they are approached by six companies every year and receive an average of one job offer.

Most executives actively practice "defensive career management." As corporate America continues to downsize, eliminating employees at all levels in the interest of productivity and profitability, executives have become more aggressive about managing their own careers. Three-quarters of executives surveyed said they tried to stay aware of alternative job prospects—even if they had no intention of changing positions. Nearly 80 percent do so as part of their "career management strategy." The survey results confirm that individual career management is now widespread and systematic, and that executives spend a significant portion of time directing their own career path.

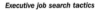

Executive job search tactics

I try to stay aware of alternative job prospects, even if I have no real intention of changing positions.
74%
13%
13%

I try to stay aware of alternative job prospects as part of my personal career management strategy.
78%
14%
8%

I try to stay aware of my alternative job prospects mainly to improve my bargaining power with my current employer.
10%
21%
69%

I often think about qutting my present job.
25%
19%
56%

I will probably look for a new job in the next year.
48%
18%
34%

Percent of respondents who:

Agree or Srongly Agree   Neither Agree nor Disagree   Disagree or Strongly Diagree

And most executives are no longer passive dreamers waiting for a recruiter to contact them. In fact, the Cornell research shows that most executives are exploring the job market actively:

Job exploration activity	Executives in past year
Revised resume	78%
Read position listings in professional journals/newspapers	76%
Sent copies of resume to a prospective employer	69%
Went to a job interview	64%
Talked to friends and relatives about getting a new job	63%
Talked to colleagues and co-workers about getting a job in another organization	45%
Initiated contact with a search firm to obtain a job with another employer	45%
Made telephone inquiries to a prospective employer	40%
Read a book about getting a new job	33%
Sought to transfer to new job within their organizations	22%

THE CAREER JUNGLE: EAT OR BE EATEN

The pressures of corporate America have never been more intense. As companies downsize, spin off, and merge, the executives who remain—even at the senior management level—are feeling more stress and less commitment to their current employer. Most of them have covertly entered the career market to keep abreast of market opportunities. But even though the unemployment rate sinks and management turnover rises, landing a new executive position hasn't gotten any easier. Executive recruiters control access to a majority of the executive positions in corporate America and, increasingly, the world. For anyone who is really serious about a new executive job, it makes sense to understand how recruiters work, what they're looking for, and how they judge your hard and soft skills—otherwise known as leadership presence.

4

WHEN THE HEADHUNTER CALLS

*By providing the recruiter the information he or she needs
at each stage of the search—and in the desired format—
executive aspirants significantly enhance their opportunities.*

Executive search is not rocket science. At its most primitive, search is a pay-as-you-go service for poaching management talent from other companies. At its most elegant, search is a professional service that can help companies:

- define the kind of management talent they need for a specific situation;
- advise them about the availability of this talent on the open market;
- recommend potential candidates who fit the bill;
- discreetly secure the confidential interest of the most qualified in making a job switch.

There are two kinds of executive search firms: contingency firms, which bill the client only if and when they fill a position, and retained firms, which require payment regardless of the search's outcome. The processes these firms follow to pinpoint and recommend candidates are quite different. Contingency firms work quickly to assemble resumes and pass them along to their clients, typically without screening or reference checking. Retainer search firms gradually assemble a slate of pre-screened, reference-checked candidates before presenting them to the client, sequentially or as a slate. Retained recruiters handle most search assignments at the senior executive level—those that pay $100,000 or more. The distinction between contingency and retained is not always clear-cut. Some retainer firms occasionally take contingency assignments, and contingency firms sometimes wangle retainer fees from the clients.

FINDING MANAGEMENT TALENT—FAST

Companies pay recruiters to find executives quickly. The majority of search assignments are completed—offer letter issued to a candidate—120 days from the date the recruiter "picks it up," according to Scott Scanlon, publisher of *Executive Search Review*. The first ten weeks of any search are usually devoted to defining the position, identifying hundreds of possible prospects, and winnowing the field to ten or twenty likely candidates who are screened over the phone.

This means the recruiter has around three weeks to personally interview four to six of the best qualified candidates, explore their resume claims, and assess their personalities, brainpower, and "chemistry" with the client. Most recruiters present four to six of these candidates to their clients, accompanied or preceded by lengthy "writeups" documenting the candidate's employment history, accomplishments, and personal attributes—and assessing how well he or she fits the position "spec."

Most executive recruiters wouldn't argue with the academics and consultants who have probed leadership. But given the time pressures of identifying, recruiting, and recommending talented executives for needy companies, recruiters don't have the time, inclination, or permission to conduct psychological tests or prepare complex longitudinal analyses.

Search isn't cheap. The rate for a single recruiting assignment is one-third of the candidate's first year compensation—base salary, bonus, signing bonus, and stock options. For recruiting an executive whose base compensation and bonuses total $300,000, the search firm receives a $100,000 payment. Often, clients can negotiate a lower fee percentage if they give the search firm multiple assignments. Today's cutthroat environment has spawned all kinds of hybrids, including partial retainers and "containers," which provide an initial retainer payment but no final fee until the candidate shows up for work.

Whether practitioners of primitive or elegant search, most retained search consultants practice their trade according to five basic steps:

1. Collecting information on the client's need and documenting it in a position description
2. Identifying prospective candidates and qualifying them through telephone screening
3. Interviewing candidates in person

4. Presenting an assessment of recommended candidates to the client in writing
5. Checking references

Executive recruiters are busy people. Typically, they are juggling a half dozen search assignments at any given time, as well as trying to sell new business. Retained recruiters, who are compensated for sales—not completed assignments—are constantly preoccupied with "picking up" assignments. Although most recruiters know that a satisfied client is the best source of additional business, many have a scarcity mentality that constantly motivates them to find fresh clients and new work. As a result, candidates who make a recruiter's life easy will float faster to the top of the recommended list—assuming the basic qualifications are met. By providing the recruiter the information he or she needs at each stage of the search—and in the desired format—executive aspirants can curry the favor of the headhunter and significantly enhance their positioning on the search assignment.

PHASE 1: WHAT DOES THE CLIENT WANT?

Executive search assignments begin when a recruiter meets with a client company to "pick up" an assignment. If the client is new, the recruiter will spend time—often hours—with the hiring manager, the company's human resources executive, and others in the organization. The purpose? To gain enough information about the company's strategic situation, corporate culture, reporting relationships, and the specific objectives and responsibilities of the position to prepare a position description.

The Position Specification

The position specification provides written marching orders for filling the executive position and serves a variety of purposes. For candidates, it:

- Provides background information on the client company, its distinctive competence, strengths and weaknesses, strategic direction, and culture.
- Describes the position, its major functions, role within the organization, responsibilities, and span of control.
- Details the experience, expertise, skills, education, and intangible factors *required* for any candidates considered for the job.
- Details the experience, expertise, skills, education, and intangible factors *desired* for any candidates considered for the job.
- Serves as a template for the written analysis the recruiter will provide for every candidate he or she sends along to the client for a personal interview.

Smith and Jones Executive Search Associates

CONFIDENTIAL POSITION SPECIFICATION

POSITION

Senior Vice President of Marketing

COMPANY

A major international assurance, tax, and consulting firm, widely respected for its strength in serving clients of all sizes, and representing a broad industry mix. With nearly $9 billion in global revenues generated through offices located in 150 countries, our client works with many of the best companies in business today.

Operating revenues of $3.8 billion in the U.S. firm represent a 27 percent increase over the prior year. Assurance and tax revenues have grown by 13 percent and 21 percent respectively during the same period. The firm is expecting to exceed 30 percent growth for fiscal year 1999. Our client's professionals are driven by a singular ambition: to electrify clients with successful, cutting-edge solutions to their business operations, thereby raising their level of performance and results. Correspondingly, the organization is intent on having a marketing unit that mirrors the firm's world class image.

REPORTING
RELATIONSHIPS

The vice president of marketing manages six assistant vice presidents and reports to the executive vice president of marketing and sales. In addition, this position will have significant matrixed reporting relationships to the area management leadership team (area managing partners), revenue team leaders, office managing partners, and all product and service leaders.

EDUCATION

Candidates must have a bachelor's degree, preferably in marketing or communications. MBA in marketing is required.

REQUIREMENTS The successful candidate should have 10 to 15 years of progressively responsible marketing or communications experience, with a significant portion at the management level.

The individual must project great professional credibility, high personal ethics, and an appreciation for the strategic ramifications of his/her decisions. The self-starter, take-charge leader we seek must be viewed as hardworking, no-nonsense, bright, and well-grounded, with an ability to garner the respect of partners and managers within the firm; someone who is both achievement- and performance-oriented.

The candidate must have an ability to work well in a highly matrixed organization where change occurs frequently; deliver results to, and through, many organizational leaders with varied demands and priorities; perform in an environment where marketing activities will have a measurable impact on firmwide financial performance and a positive effect on the marketplace. The candidate must be able to provide true value to client engagements and create value for clients and their customers.

Service sector experience is highly valued, but not required, for this role. Prior contact with large professional services firms is desirable.

An ability to live the organization's core values of open and honest communications, personal accountability, strong leadership, breadth of knowledge, teamwork, and a collaborative style are extremely important. In addition, providing an environment where open, constructive dialogue exists in building solutions for clients, whether internally or externally, is vital.

RESPONSIBILITIES The successful candidate will have day-to-day responsibility for a staff of 15 to 20 managers and staff personnel covering a broad range of marketing-related areas.

Oversight of the regional implementation of national marketing programs will be of primary concern to the Senior Vice President of Marketing. Participation on a national team providing strategy development input leading to the national programs is essential and expected. By working closely with the various line product and service line leaders and industry leaders, the Senior Vice President of Marketing will gain the necessary knowledge capital regarding the strategic direction of the practice to provide appropriate marketing support.

The Senior Vice President of Marketing will also be charged with providing counsel to partners and managers on developing tactical marketing programs to reach the target audience in an effort to expand both the firm's service offerings and reach. This local strategy development will begin with customer relationship development and continue through the selling of engagement-related services.

In addition to the responsibilities listed above, the successful candidate will also need to:

Build and manage a regional marketing team providing the energy, drive, and focus to reach the firm's expectations for profitability within the region. This includes leadership in the hiring, training, and retention of key marketing personnel.

Create a culture that emphasizes commitment to the organization's core values where deliverables and activities will be on time, focused, developed in a collaborative environment, with the utmost dedication to quality.

Provide strategic direction and implement leadership relative to community and public relations activities in the region's various offices including alumni relations and charitable activities.

Generate creative design and implement ideas for sales programs, event management programs, and regional brand management initiatives. This includes overseeing the field-marketing implementation as necessary.

Develop and manage the area marketing budget, providing oversight and control of firm resources. Insure a dynamic planning process to allocate the capital effectively and efficiently.

Build the marketing relationships between each of the practice units in order to create and maintain a consistent world-class firm image.

PERSONAL
QUALITIES   Our client is seeking a highly analytical, strategic thinker with good listening and communication skills. In addition, the position requires an individual who takes considerable initiative in generating and packaging new products as well as working with sales and marketing professionals.

COMPENSATION   Our client is prepared to extend an attractive compensation package based on level of achievement, plus bonus eligibility. In addition, the firm offers a superior employee benefits package. If required, a relocation package will be provided.

PHASE 2—IDENTIFYING AND QUALIFYING PROSPECTIVE CANDIDATES

The recruiter who picks up the search may not be the one who actually handles the heavy lifting—digging up and qualifying a pool of candidates who meet the "specs" for the position. That task often falls to junior associates who spend their time scouring the Internet or networking on the phone to generate a list of fifteen to twenty individuals who meet the basic "hard" requirements of the job—years of experience, industry expertise, etc.

Unless you are a top executive at a major public company, you're likely to hear first about the search over the phone from the associate, who is also responsible for qualifying your hard skills and passing you up the food chain. You'll be told that the firm is conducting a search for the position, given a broad-brush description of the firm's client and the position in question, and asked if you know anyone who might qualify—a backhanded way to get you to volunteer yourself.

Telephone Screening

If you sound interested, the recruiter will screen you over the phone by requesting your resume or reviewing your career history, major accomplishments, and education. At this stage, the search firm is after basics. They will listen closely for evidence of your poise, manners, and communication skills.

Whether or not to fax a resume immediately is a subject of debate among recruiters. Maintaining a current resume is nothing more than prudence and common sense, according to David R. Peasback, chairman and CEO of recruiter Canny, Bowen Inc. As recently as five to ten years ago, recruiters would look with some suspicion on an individual who offered to fax or mail an updated resume on little or no notice. "This was a possible red flag, indicating that the individual was perhaps on shaky ground in his or her present company or perhaps already engaged in an active, if discreet, job search," says Peasback. But with all of the turmoil in corporate life over the last several years, recruiters are now more likely to view a current resume as practical. "Recruiters are usually working under tremendous time pressures in trying to fill a search, they will appreciate a readily available summary of your background and accomplishments, rather than having to painstakingly cover all of this information in an extended telephone conversation," advises Peasback.

The Resume Debate

On the other hand, most recruiters and clients are more comfortable with candidates who are gainfully employed and not looking for a new job, according to Skott Burkland, president of Skott/Edwards Consultants. "In the United States, as opposed to Europe, few gainfully employed, secure, happy people keep a resume up to date. They may have a one-paragraph backgrounder, but they rarely have a comprehensive curriculum vitae." According to Burkland, "Those who have their credentials ready to forward to a recruiter are those who are already looking or considering a job change. And the more senior the position, the more likely the case. Anyone who sends me a current resume right away makes me wonder why he or she is looking."

Perhaps the best strategy is to ask the recruiter to send you a copy of the position specification before you forward your resume. That way, you'll have a chance to reflect on whether you're seriously interested in the position, if only overnight, and tailor your own resume accordingly. In addition, you'll avoid appearing too eager. Even if the recruiter is in a hurry, a twenty-four-hour delay won't generally put you out of contention.

Once eight to ten prospects are screened, the recruiter and his or her associate will arrange a personal interview with the four to six who appear to be best qualified for the position.

PHASE 3: THE PERSONAL INTERVIEW

As unemployment hovers at historic lows and managers spin faster than ever through corporate America's revolving doors, companies are hard pressed to find management talent. But executive recruiters don't invite candidates to a personal interview unless they meet certain minimum standards and could conceivably be hired. Today, when experience means less and companies hire primarily for potential, resumes don't tell companies what they need to know. "People create a new edition of their resume for each job interview," says Fred Siegel, CEO of headhunter Conex Incorporated. "That's why my clients and I take personal meetings a lot more seriously than before."

Headhunters spend an inordinate amount of time in airports. Occasionally, they're flying to meet a client. But most frequently, they're interviewing candidates. Chicago's O'Hare Airport and the Dallas-Fort Worth International Airport are two of the biggest headhunter meeting points. Centrally located, they enable recruiters from major metropolitan areas to conduct two-hour assessments of candidates from smaller towns or the opposite coast in a discreet, fast, and inexpensive manner.

Despite the growth of videoconferencing, most recruiters prefer to meet a candidate in the flesh. Although personal interviews are time-consuming and expensive, they're essential for preventing disasters. In one search, recruiter Don Clark, a partner with Ray & Berndtson, was relieved he had made the trek to O'Hare for a personal interview. The candidate's background, experience, and education were exactly what the company wanted for its new executive vice president. "On paper, there was no better match," says Clark. "But after interviewing him in person, we knew we'd have to keep looking. The candidate didn't look or act like an executive. What's worse, he lectured me for forty-five minutes on what my client was doing wrong and why he was just the man to fix the problem."

According to Clark, the candidate's rumpled suit, dirty shoes, poor posture, and big mouth cost him the job.

> *An interview is your time as well as mine. I'm here to learn about you but also to help you understand my client better. Outline for me aspects of your background that you want me and my client to know. My expectations for you are that you will be well prepared, demonstrate energy and freshness, and speak in a confident, positive way about what you've done.*
> NORM MITCHELL, VICE PRESIDENT, A.T. KEARNEY EXECUTIVE SEARCH

The Ultimate Test
No longer a perfunctory chitchat session, the interview has become the ultimate test of a candidate's suitability. This is where a candidate's appearance, behavior, passion, charisma, communication skills, intellect, and fit

with the company's culture are scrutinized and evaluated. "We want a candidate to look good, sound good, stay cool, have a sense of humor, stay balanced, have a value structure, be on time, let the discussion be 50-50, and ask about the next step," says Gerry Roche. "We don't want candidates to get too linear, dump on their old company or be negative." It's also the place where the candidate's "closeability" is tested. "The candidate may have great qualifications, but if he or she doesn't appear interested, we won't make a positive recommendation to our client," says a Chicago-based recruiter.

Some candidates come to an interview assuming that the recruiter is going to draw them out. Others make grandiose claims like, "We had a problem in finance and I fixed it," without providing any evidence or examples. This makes recruiters suspicious as to whether the person is truly a capable contributor. The best people want to have a mutually beneficial business discussion.

According to Herman Smith, chairman of EMA Partners, there's a hierarchy at work in the executive interview process. "Recruiters look for both threshold and higher-order factors when evaluating leadership presence," says Smith. "At the very bottom are essential needs: punctuality and a well-groomed appearance. The next level includes preparation, listening skills, and having a kindly bearing. Then comes the ability to think on your feet, strategize, discuss concepts, build on other people's concepts, and synthesize information. Finally, there's emotional intelligence."

Essentials

All employees, from receptionist to CEO, need to be reliable, credible, and capable of functioning with other people.

What recruiters look for: on time arrival, grooming, demeanor, manners, and basic communication skills, including the ability to carry on a two-way conversation, pay attention to what's being said, and respond in a clear manner.

> *Key cues:* *How you look*
> *How you behave*
> *What you say*
> *How you say it*

Conceptual Skills

In addition to the essentials, managers and professionals need to demonstrate general intellectual competence and emotional intelligence.

What recruiters look for: ability to "think on their feet," discuss concepts and draw conclusions from changing premises, awareness of the needs of multiple stakeholders, breadth and precision of vocabulary, sense of humor.

> *Key cues:* *What you say*
> *How you say it*
> *How you think*

Leadership Skills

Higher-level managers must understand how to achieve goals and what the tradeoffs are in attaining them.

What recruiters look for: evidence that candidates were responsible for past achievements, not merely beneficiaries; candidate's specific role in accomplishments; how they handled challenges, overcame failures, and united people to attain goals. "Some of my candidates are members of the _lucky sperm club_," says Brian Sullivan, president and CEO of recruiters Sullivan & Co. "They were raised in wealth, attended the right schools, and have great pedigrees. My job is to confirm that they haven't simply had their accomplishments handed to them."

> Key cues: *What you say*
>   *How you say it*
>   *How you think*
>   *Charisma*
>   *Culture fit*

Vision

Vision is the hallmark of top executives, and one of the most difficult factors to confirm on paper or even in person. "Most recruiters don't have the brainpower to be visionaries but they can recognize it," says Herman Smith. "Some of my clients and candidates think on a higher level than I do. I don't necessarily have to understand what they're saying, but I have to judge their ability to create a vision."

What recruiters look for: ability to discuss the multiple forces affecting current employer's performance, including competition, customers, employees, technological change; willingness to admit failures and discuss what he/she learned from them; insight into recruiting company's strategic challenges and options for addressing them.

> Key cues: *How you think*
>   *Charisma*
>   *Passion*

PHASE 4: CANDIDATE ASSESSMENT

Even the best-qualified candidates won't get offers if they bungle the recruiter interview. Candidates who turn in a lackluster performance on two or more leadership presence criteria are crossed off the list. The recruiters who provided input for this book indicated an average interview "ding" rate of 30 to 40 percent—they recommend fewer than three of every every five candidates whom they interview in person.

If you are one of the 60 percent who make it through the recruiter interview, you will be "written up" in a formal assessment for the client. Recruiters typically dictate the key points for these assessments on the plane ride back from their interview with you, and their assistants fill in the prosaic details. Most executive recruiting firms structure their candidate assessments in three key sections:

Career brief. Your resume, reformatted in the search firm's signature style.

Appraisal. A four- to six-page discussion of candidate qualifications and accomplishments against client requirements. Some recruiters incorporate executive presence into this communication; others create a separate attachment highlighting presence factors.

Compensation summary. A two-paragraph description of your current compensation package, including perks and any special benefits you might currently have.

Smith and Jones Executive Search Associates

CONFIDENTIAL CANDIDATE ASSESSMENT

Part 1: Career Brief

David W. Jensen
45 Rue de la Paix
Neuilly F-75008 France

011-33-1-48.44.74.81 (home)
011-33-1-54.76.98.12 (office)

EDUCATION

1973	B.A.	University of Pennsylvania
1975	M.B.A.	Wharton School, University of Pennsylvania
1975	C.P. A.	Pennsylvania

EXPERIENCE

1983–present   WORLDWIDE FOODS, INC.
Worldwide is a $3.5 billion food and restaurant company. Headquartered in New York, the company has operations in 27 countries worldwide, including the Whatachicken restaurant chain.

1989–present   **Regional Finance Director, Whatachicken, Paris**
Responsible for all financial functions of 600 restaurants in Europe, the Middle East, and Africa with total sales of $600 million.
Jensen reports to Whatachicken's regional vice president for Europe, Middle East, and Africa. His major responsibilities include:

* Financial reporting and forecasting.
* Developing annual operating plans.
* Coordinating the strategic planning program for the region.

* Coordinating with corporate tax and treasury organization in New York.
* Merger and acquisition analysis, restructuring existing joint ventures, and business development (approximately 30% of time).

Jensen's direct reports include three managers over planning, control, and development. His indirect reports include four regional financial directors.

1987–1989	**Director of Planning, New York**

Responsible for strategic and operating plans of Worldwide's 12 overseas operating companies. Jensen reported to Worldwide's chief financial officer and supervised a staff of four. He modeled financials and analyzed data for the companies and worked closely with top management in valuation, merger and acquisition activities, including the Jones Crisps and Hospitality Foods mergers.

1985–1987　**Controller, New York**

Responsible for control and financial reporting functions of company's Eurasian division, $1.5 billion in sales. Reporting to the vice president of finance, Jensen managed a staff of six and was responsible for 10 controllers within 10 operating companies outside the U.S.

1975–1985　**ARTHUR ANDERSEN, Chicago**

1983–1985　**Director of Domestic Audit, Worldwide Foods**

Reporting to Andersen's regional audit committee, Jensen managed the annual audit for Worldwide.

1981–1983　**Senior Manager, Oil and Gas Operations**

Reporting to the national oil and gas practice director, Jensen managed several audits at oil and gas corporations.

1975–1981　Various positions, including staff auditor, auditor in charge, senior auditor, supervisor.

Part 2: Candidate Assessment

David W. Jensen

David Jensen has a solid grounding in corporate accounting and control functions. While controller for Worldwide Foods' Eurasian division from 1985–1987, he was responsible for accounting, tax, treasury, control and financial reporting. Some of his activities in this position are similar to those required in the Consolidated position. For example, he standardized accounting policies, developed case and tax management systems for each country in the Worldwide Foods' Eurasian domain, and developed a number of consolidated reports that allowed his supervisors to analyze the operations of the international companies. This experience would allow him to "hit the ground running" in the Consolidated position.

Jensen's strong professional skills are evident in his rapid career path at Arthur Andersen. He joined the firm in 1975 after obtaining an M.B.A. and progressed through the positions of staff auditor, auditor in charge, senior auditor, supervisor and, in 1981, manager. He acquired valuable experience working with banks, financial services, and insurance companies—experience that proved extremely useful later in his career as he established banking relationships worldwide. In 1981, he became senior manager of oil and gas operations at the firm's headquarters in Chicago and broadened his skills with some marketing experience: his responsibilities centered around developing products and series that could be offered to Arthur Andersen's oil field services clients. He monitored the technical development of the oil and gas staff and prepared publications and training materials to support Andersen's competitive position as a provider of audit on the Worldwide Foods account, and was subsequently invited to join Worldwide as controller of the Eurasian division in 1985.

Jensen clearly has a strong track record in strategic planning, investment, operational analysis, and liaison work with operating company management—all key requirements for the Consolidated position. He has solid professional training and certification, and is a capable controller who has shown the ability to structure and manage a complex international financial network successfully. His involvement with numerous acquisition, divestiture, and joint venture projects at Worldwide reflects his ability to address key strategic issues and work closely with top management.

Although Jensen's experience and capabilities seem ideally suited for the Consolidated position, a concern is his relative lack of experience with startup companies. He came into his current position with the 600-restaurant network already up and operating. His activities have focused on streamlining accounting and treasury functions, establishing strong financial systems, managing budgeting, and planning processes for mature successful operations. Although Whatachicken and Worldwide have made acquisitions, they have been relatively minor additions to the corporate product line. Jensen appears to be capable of handling the challenge of a startup or new product situation, but he is untested in this area.

Another concern we have is Jensen's willingness to live in Indianapolis. Jensen and his family are quite happy in Paris. He speaks French well and, having lived for the past nine years in large, sophisticated metropolitan areas, is concerned about a move to a smaller city. Although Jensen has the personality, style, and experience to work successfully with you and Consolidated's team-oriented culture, he may find Indianapolis somewhat provincial and isolated.

Overall, we believe that Jensen's strengths and potential offer a unique fit with Consolidated's needs for a vice president–international. We believe that with an appropriate compensation package, he could be attracted to your company and adjust well to the change in location.

Part 3: Compensation Summary

David W. Jensen

Jensen is currently earning a base salary of $220,000. In 1993 he received a bonus of $136,000. He participates in Worldwide Foods' stock option program, and earns $175,000 in stock options annually. He also receives incentive stock units that vest over a three-year period. The company provides him with a car.

Client Review

After reviewing the candidate assessment, the recruiter's client can take one of three actions:

- Interview the candidate immediately (80 percent of cases);
- Interview the candidate when the recruiter has completed assessments of all final candidates (18 percent of cases);
- Reject the candidate, despite the recruiter's recommendation, without an interview (2 percent of cases).

While a search firm can recommend an executive and make a strong case for hiring, the client is the ultimate decision-maker, and the level of trust between the client and the recruiter, along with the sensitivity of the position, will determine the next step. Occasionally, a client requires only a simple meeting with the candidate and extends an employment offer immediately. In most cases, the candidate will be brought into the client's headquarters for a day of interviews with potential peers, bosses, and employees. In CEO searches, candidates typically meet with the organization's board as a group as well as one on one with key directors. In the past, companies have required psychological testing or other screens beyond the recruiter's recommendation. However, the shortage of qualified executives and their increasing unwillingness to submit to assessments has caused a decline in executive testing.

PHASE 5: FINAL REFERENCE CHECKING

References are the recruiter's most important tool, according to Dayton Ogden, president of Spencer Stuart, who conducts searches mainly at the CEO, board, and top executive levels. "CEOs aren't selected by boards for their job history as much as for their leadership ability. No one gets near a search committee unless he or she has the technical skills and intellectual apparatus to do the job," says Ogden. "At the CEO level, companies are looking for someone who provides a vision as well as a strong ability to deal with the people. At the level we're working, the best source of information about a candidate's ability to do the job and executive presence are people who've worked with them before."

Like most recruiters, Ogden asks candidates to provide the names of four or five individuals who can comment on their capabilities and management style. Knowing that candidates almost always suggest their friends or people who will provide glowing recommendations, Ogden often asks candidates to provide several adversarial references—people with whom they have had significant conflict—as well. "I want to get the full story. I need to know how they handle conflict, deal with opposing viewpoints, and whether they treat antagonists with respect," he says. Do candidates resist? Says Ogden, "In my experience, the ones with the greatest confidence not only give me names, but they are most likely to say, 'That's a terrific idea. Have at 'em.'"

The best recruiters, like Ogden, won't stop at the names provided by the candidate. They will also reference the references to determine the nature and extent of their relationship with the candidate. Then they'll continue digging, asking the references for additional names, branching out to build a fully developed portrait of the candidate in action.

Smith and Jones Executive Search Associates
Sample Reference Report

Subject: Peter W. Harrison

Date: March 5, 1999

Reference: S. T. McDay
                Chairman of the Board
                Dakota Gulf Bancshares, Inc.
                P.O. Box 1498
                Lake Jackson, ND 57566
                709/265-8191(O)
                709/297-5124 (H)

S. T. McDay has known Harrison since he was 12 years old. McDay has served as the holding company's chairman since 1988 and was a bank customer for over 10 years.

The following is a summary of McDay's remarks during a conversation with our firm on March 4, 1999.

McDay feels that Harrison has "one of the most intelligent banking and investment minds" to which he has been exposed. He adds that Harrison is astute, dignified, reserved, organized, and professional. He believes he could be more outgoing, yet his marketing skills are good. One of his primary strengths is his ability to "research problems and successfully solve them."

McDay said that Harrison has "done a great job of tactfully balancing a board member that represents controlling interest in the company who is often difficult to work with." As a manager, Harrison totally stands behind his people and is stern but fair. Harrison evidently takes direction well and "you won't catch him off guard because he will research your direction."

He mentions that Harrison has several friends socially and has harnessed a tremendous amount of respect professionally. He is "family-oriented with high character."

WORKING WITH EXECUTIVE RECRUITERS— THE SEVEN COMMANDMENTS

As you plot your professional trajectory, it's a near certainty that one or more of your career moves will be prompted by a call from an executive recruiter. Now that you understand the five-stage process that recruiters use to fill executive positions, keep seven rules in mind when you become a headhunter's quarry:

1. *Take their calls.* You never know. After he was fired from Ford, Lee Iacocca was an out-of-work executive wondering if he would ever see the inside of another company when a recruiter called him about working for Chrysler. And many happily employed executives have been surprised to learn that there are better career opportunities available.

2. *Know who's doing what.* Get to know the associate or junior partner who is handling your assignment—not just the big-name partner who may have called you initially. Big search firms typically operate on a two-tier system, with partners handling client contact and selling. For all assignments except CEOs and other top positions, junior associates typically handle the legwork, including initial contact with candidates, providing position descriptions and initial information, scheduling appointments, and keeping track of the assignment's status. The senior partner typically interviews finalists, after being briefed by the associates, and one or the other will complete the actual writeup forwarded to the client. Junior associates typically conduct reference calls on all but CEO and high-level assignments.

3. *Request the position specification.* Always ask the recruiter to send you the written position specification before expressing interest in a search assignment. If the client is a public company, the recruiter should also send you a copy of its annual report, 10-K, and marketing materials.

4. *Never fax your resume on demand.* You need to see the position specification to customize your resume for the situation at hand. Wait a few days, and if you're still interested in the position, tailor your resume to match the job requirement before sending it.

5. *Don't assume you're being offered a job.* Many are called in the course of a search, but few are chosen. Anyone who appears too eager reduces his or her desirability, say most recruiters.

6. *Be prepared.* When you meet with a recruiter in person, you should have a firm fix on how to frame your background to best attract the recruiter's interest, and that of his or her client. Use the advice offered throughout this book to build your story most effectively and act the part.

7. *You're on stage all the time.* Don't assume that recruiters or employers aren't listening if they stop taking notes. Some headhunters pride themselves on generating confidential, personal information through "stealth" interviews over meals where candidates tend to lower their guard. "When I put my notepad away, candidates say amazing things," says Bob Clarke, principal with recruiters Furst Group/MPI. "That's when they're likely to run down their current employer, drop names inappropriately, or even use foul language."

5

DO YOU HAVE LEADERSHIP PRESENCE?

An informal questionnaire to measure how your leadership presence stacks up.

Your professional accomplishments are only the minimum requirement for landing a new executive job. When companies have to choose between two equally qualified candidates, leadership presence is always the deciding factor, according to recruiters. Scrutinizing, understanding, and developing your leadership presence is critical to thriving in your organization's environment—whether it's your current company or a new organization. Answer all the questions—honestly—and compare your scores with benchmarks suggested by top recruiters.

1. **Number of times you have been promoted in the last five years _____.**
2. **Number of times per year you are called by an executive recruiter _____.**

3.   **Which category best describes your wardrobe?**

Men
Brooks Brothers
Armani
Land's End

Women
Ann Taylor
Talbot's
Armani

4.   **Check the categories that best describe your hair:**

Men
Gray or going gray
Receding hairline
What hair?
Mustache
Beard

Women
Chin length or shorter
Shoulder length
Below shoulder length

5.   **Business accessories (check all that apply):**
Dark leather briefcase
Naugahyde briefcase
Canvas briefcase
Don't use briefcase
Designer pen
Ordinary ballpoint pen
Felt tip pen

6. **Personal accessories (check all that apply):**
Silk scarf
Hermes-style tie
Tie clip
Clip or post earrings
Dangling earrings
Monogrammed pin
Class ring
Cuff links
Wristwatch
Bracelet

7. **Best menu choices for a business lunch (select all that apply):**
Onion soup
Caesar salad
Pasta
Grilled fish
Merlot
Rack of lamb
Baked potato

8. **Select the best sentence:**
a. At the last meeting, the chairman explained the restructuring program to the board and I.
b. The restructuring program was announced by the chairman at the last meeting.
c. The chairman explained the restructuring program to the board and me at the last meeting.
d. The chairman told the board and I about the restructuring program at the last meeting.

9. **Books you have read in the last six months:**

_____
_____
_____

10. **Publications you regularly read (select all that apply):**
    The Wall Street Journal
    Fortune
    Forbes
    Newsweek
    Time
    Harvard Business Review
    Local newspaper

11. **How do you typically communicate an important announcement to employees? (Select two):**
    Written memo
    E-mail
    Videotape
    One-on-one
    Telephone
    Speech

12. **The most important aspects of communicating well are (select two):**
    Focusing on the big picture
    Listening
    Spelling out all the details clearly
    Telling everyone, from top executives to
       receptionists, the same thing
    Connecting with people

13. **You like talking about (choose one):**
    Mistakes you have made
    Your accomplishments
    What worries you

14. **When speaking about a concept or program you support, you like to (select all that apply):**
    Quote business thinkers or historical figures
    Use logic
    Use emotion
    Talk for 10 minutes or less

Ask your audience to "picture" something
Ask rhetorical questions and answer them

15. **You worry most about (choose one):**
     ✓Your current competitors
     Your future competitors

16. **You like to communicate a complex idea by using (choose one):**
     ✓A one-page memo
     A 5-10 page memo
     A one-page chart
     You find props and charts get in the way

17. **Some of the things you enjoy most are (select all that apply):**
     ✓Having lunch with employees to find out what's going on
     Walking the halls to find out what's going on
     ✓The company's annual Christmas party
     One-on-one discussions with thoughtful people
     Having some peace and quiet in your office
     Mixing it up with the board of directors
     Talking to reporters

18. **In the last six months, how many times have you made a speech/presentation to a group of more than ten people?**
     More than three times
     Two to three times
     One or zero times

19. **When you speak, people can tell you're from (choose one):**
     The South or Midwest
     The New York City area
     Other U.S. region
     ✓Outside the U.S.
     ✗ They can't tell

20. **When traveling, you call your office:**
Once a day
Three times a day
Every hour

21. **Describe your greatest career accomplishment.**

_____

_____

_____

22. **Name a business leader you admire and emulate.**

_____

23. **Describe your greatest weaknesses.**

_____

_____

_____

24. **Name three things you learned from a recent negative experience.**

_____

_____

_____

25. **What would your boss say about you?**

_____

_____

_____

26. **What do you most like/dislike about your current job?**

_____

_____

_____

Interpreting the scores

1. **Promotions**
   Once = 1 point   More than once = 3 points

   Research by Cornell University's Center for Advanced Human
   Resources Studies and search firm Ray & Berndtson shows
   that the typical recruitable executive is promoted every 3.5
   years. Promotions are highly correlated with perceived
   executive presence.

2. **Recruiter calls**
   1 to 3 times = 1 point   4 to 7 times = 2 points
   8+ times = 3 points

   The same research found that the typical recruitable executive
   receives an average of six calls per year from headhunters.

3. **Wardrobe**
   Men
   Brooks Brothers   = 2 points
   Armani   = 0 points
   Land's End   = 0 points

   Although appropriate attire varies from industry to industry,
   most top executives wear well-made, classic clothing but avoid
   looking like they stepped out of the pages of GQ.

   Women
   Ann Taylor   = 1 point
   Talbot's   = 2 points
   Armani   = 0 points

   Clothing is trickier for female executives. Most prefer the
   middlebrow, tailored look found in the suit section of the
   Talbot's catalogue, rather than an ultra-fashionable look. Ann
   Taylor clothes tend to be cut short and slim and are best for
   women under the age of thirty.

4. **Hair**

Men

Gray or going gray	= 2 points
Receding hairline	= 1 point
What hair?	= 0 points
Mustache	= 0 points
Beard	= -1 point

Most recruiters say graying temples suggest sagacity and experience, as does a receding hairline, to a lesser degree. Beards are viewed with suspicion. Many recruiters think men who have them are trying to make a statement about their education and intellect, or hiding part of their face—covering up something.

Women

Chin length or shorter	= 2 points
Shoulder length	= 2 points
Below shoulder length	= 0 points

Women tend to wear their hair long between puberty and adulthood, and long hair makes female executives seem less authoritative unless they pull it back in a chignon. Most recruiters suggest that women cut their hair to shoulder length or shorter to be taken more seriously in a business setting. Although some recruiters claim that graying hair on a woman doesn't suggest wisdom and experience as it does for men, most said that gray or colored hair were equally acceptable, provided that colored hair is natural looking and touched up regularly.

5. **Business accessories**

Dark leather briefcase	= 2 points
Naugahyde briefcase	= -1 point
Canvas briefcase	= -1 point
Don't use briefcase	= 0 points

Designer pen	=	2 points
Ordinary ballpoint pen	=	0 points
Felt tip pen	=	-1 point

Your business accessories declare your status. Most executives carry fine leather briefcases and use Mont Blanc, Cartier, or other fine pens. Felt tip pens brand you as an order taker.

6. Personal accessories

Hermes-style tie	=	2 points
Tie clip	=	-1 point
Class ring	=	-1 point
Cuff links	=	1 point
Silk scarf	=	2 points
Clip or post earrings	=	1 point
Dangling earrings	=	-1 point
Monogrammed pin	=	-1 point
Bracelet	=	1 point
Wristwatch	=	1 point

An elegant silk tie can dramatically enhance an ordinary navy blue suit. Most recruiters recognize that Hermes, Ferragamo, or Gucci ties are preferred by senior executives and closely examine the ties that their candidates wear. Tie clips are passé. Large class or fraternity rings detract from your executive presence, but an attractive pair of cuff links makes a positive statement.

For women, a silk scarf, artfully tied or draped, is an elegant, sophisticated accessory. Earrings are an enhancement, but be sure yours are the clip or post style. Earrings that swing scream "party time." Anything with your initials on it—or a designer's initials—is inappropriate. A single bangle bracelet in silver or gold is a tasteful addition. Both men and women should wear a good quality wristwatch.

7. Lunch choices

Onion soup	= 0 points
Caesar salad	= 0 points

Pasta	=	0 points
Grilled fish	=	2 points
Merlot	=	-1 point
Rack of lamb	=	0 points
Baked potato	=	0 points

It's best to avoid interviewing over meals if possible—particularly a first interview with a recruiter. Talking seriously, maintaining poise, and carving or manipulating food—other than to put it in your mouth—are too many activities to juggle at once. If you must eat and meet, order something simple and avoid multiple plates and courses. The fish is the only safe choice on the list. Select foods that can be eaten with a fork. Onion soup and pastas are too drippy. Caesar salad is messy and requires cutting up to eat gracefully. Any meat with a bone should be avoided because carving is distracting and messy. A baked potato requires too much manipulation at the table. Avoid alcoholic beverages at lunchtime; a glass of wine is acceptable at dinner.

8. **Best sentence**
   a, d = -1 point   b= 0 points   c= 2 points

   Sentences b and c are grammatically correct, but good communicators avoid using the passive voice in oral and written communications. Don't fall into the trap of trying to appear too correct by using the nominative case as the object of a preposition, as in sentences a and d. Instead of improving your communications, it makes you appear foolish.

9. **Books**
   Give yourself three points for every book. Senior executives sharpen their intellects, imaginations, and communication skills by reading new ideas presented in books of all kinds.

10. **Publications**
    Give yourself two points for each publication checked for the same reason as above.

11. Communicating important announcements

Give yourself two points for each item checked. While each company has its own communication traditions, in general, you can't overcommunicate—particularly on a major announcement—and the more media employed, the better the message will sink in.

12. Which aspects of communicating are most important?

Focusing on the big picture	=	1 point
Listening	=	2 points
Spelling out all the details clearly	=	0 points
Telling everyone, from top executives to receptionists, the same thing	=	-1 point
Connecting with people	=	2 points

Recruiters say listening and connecting are the keys to effective communication. While focusing on the big picture is appropriate in many instances, it's irrelevant in some situations. Although you need to be familiar with the details of a specific decision or situation, spelling them out is usually best left to an instruction manual or the manager who will be responsible for implementation. Telling everyone the same thing is not always the best way to communicate. What you say to various audiences should certainly not contradict what you tell others, but you will likely need to emphasize certain points with some audiences or provide others with more detail.

13. You like talking about (choose one)

Mistakes you have made	= 2 points
Your accomplishments	= 0 points
What worries you	= 1 point

Top executives talk about what they have learned from their mistakes. Another favorite category is issues on the horizon that concern them.

14. **When speaking about a concept or program you support, you:**

Quote business thinkers or historical figures	= 1 point
Use logic	= 0 points
Use emotion	= 1 point
Talk for ten minutes or less	= 0 points
Ask your audience to "picture" something	= 1 point
Ask rhetorical questions then answer them	= 0 points

Executives with charisma use quotes, emotion, and pictures to persuade or inspire.

15. **You worry most about**

Current competitors	= 0 points
Future competitors	= 1 point

Executives with presence are focused ten years ahead of the rest of us.

16. **Communicating a complex idea**

A one-page memo	= 0 points
A five- to ten-page page memo	= -1 point
A one-page chart	= 2 points
You find props and charts get in the way	= 0 points

Executives with charisma are master simplifiers. They like uncomplicated props or charts, and they hate lengthy reports.

17. **Things you enjoy most**

Having lunch with employees to find out what's going on	= 1 point
Walking the halls to find out what's going on	= 1 point
The company's annual Christmas party	= 0 points

One-on-one discussions with thoughtful people	= 1 point
Having some peace and quiet in your office	= 0 points
Mixing it up with the board of directors	= 1 point
Talking to reporters	= 1 point
Talking to customers	= 2 points

Executives with presence seek feedback and input from a variety of sources and make a structured effort to interact with key groups regularly. In smaller companies, they may walk the halls; in large organizations where this is impractical, they may show up on the assembly line during the third shift or make impromptu visits to various operations. Most executives attend the annual Christmas party but don't find it particularly enjoyable because the number of attendees makes it impossible to have meaningful interactions with anyone.

18. In the last six months, how many times have you made a speech/presentation to a group of more than ten people?

More than three times	= 2 points
Two to three times	= 1 point
One or zero times	= 0 points

Speaking in public enhances communication skills and helps executives sharpen their key messages.

19. When you speak, people can tell you're from (choose one):

the South or Midwest	= 0 points
the New York City area	= 1 point
Other U.S. region	= 0 points
Outside the U.S.	= 0 points
They can't tell	= 2 points

A strong southern or Midwestern accent is viewed as provincial by some recruiters. A foreign accent may raise questions about

English communications skills. A New York accent and the rapid speech that typically accompanies it can be threatening to audiences outside the Northeast. But unless you have the charisma of a Herb Kelleher, CEO of Southwest Airlines, the best way to speak is like Joe (or Joanne) from nowhere—a television news anchor.

20. When traveling, you call your office:

Once a day	= 1 point
Three times a day	= 0 points
Every hour	= -1 point

Calling too often makes it seem like you don't have anything else to do.

21. Greatest career accomplishment.

22. Business leader you most admire and emulate.

23. Greatest weaknesses.

24. Things you learned from a recent negative experience.

25. What your boss would say

Questions 21–25: One point for each answer you give, up to five items, if it includes sufficient evidence and measurable results. Executives with presence have given serious thought to these questions and have responses prepared for general use in speeches, one-on-one conversations, and even questionnaires. See Chapters 7 and 8 for more details on answering interview questions.

26. What you like/dislike.

Give yourself

-3 points for anything you say that you specifically dislike.

2 points for everything you like, up to three items

It's important to think positive: you've learned a significant amount from every experience; the issue now is, what's the missing component? What additional responsibilities, decisions do you wish you could have?

Total score

90 to 100	You're loaded with executive presence—happy landings!
70 to 90	You've made a great start—keep working at it.
below 70	Start polishing your executive presence.

6

HOW YOU
LOOK

Appearances are only skin deep. But if you don't look the
part, you won't make it to second base.

Recruiters are airport habitués. To avoid compromising
candidates or tipping off employees at a client company
that an incumbent may be replaced, many headhunters
find airports convenient and anonymous for candidate
interviews. Some of a recruiter's tensest moments take
place in airports as the plane holding their candidate pulls
up to the gate and passengers begin emerging from the jetway. "I usually stand off to the side and eyeball each person
as they come through the arrival gate," says one recruiter.
"I can hear myself saying, 'Please let it be him,' 'Thank
God—it's her,' or, 'I hope it's not him.' But by then it's too
late. I've told the candidate what I look like and we're
already shaking hands."

Most of the time, recruiters are happy with what they
see. "If we've done a good job with our initial research and

telephone screening, the physical reality is usually predictable," says Dennis Carey of Spencer Stuart. "Of course, we'd like all our candidates to be tall, attractive, suave, urbane, and brilliant. And most of the time they are."

NIGHTMARES COME TRUE

But occasionally, nightmares come true. Bob Clarke tells about a candidate he interviewed to be the top executive of a provider-sponsored startup HMO. "I spent seven months courting a physician executive. Her technical abilities were superior, and she was impressive on the phone. When I finally met her, it was the longest hour I ever spent. She wouldn't look me in the eye; her handshake was weak, she had difficulty responding to questions clearly, and her grooming left something to be desired. I didn't present her to my client because she flunked the interview."

In another search, the recruiter hadn't had an easy time finding a new division president for an office equipment manufacturer based in the Midwest. "Everyone we talked to wanted to stay on the East or West Coast," said the recruiter. "But one candidate's work history, accomplishments, and skills were spot-on. And he was someone willing to pick up and move." However, a personal meeting at O'Hare Airport's Red Carpet Club sent the recruiter back to the file cabinet. "The minute he walked off the jetway, I said, 'Dear God, I hope it's not him.'" The candidate wore a plaid sports jacket and a pink shirt. His pants hovered two inches above his scuffed shoes. He had a five o'clock shadow—at 10 A.M. in the morning—and carried a Naugahyde briefcase stuffed with ragged papers, a cellular phone, and *USA Today*. And he looked like a deer caught in the headlights. "The minute I saw this guy, I knew why he was interested in the job," says the recruiter. "He was clearly unpromotable in his current situation."

While recruiting a new CEO, Susan Bishop, president of Bishop Partners, had agreed to meet a candidate even though his resume and background were not on the mark. Although his industry knowledge was solid and he had good marketing and sales experience, he had never run a business—usually a must-have requirement for a CEO. "He was a knockout," says Bishop. "He was trim and didn't have the pot belly that men over 40 typically develop. His clothes fit him well. He was alert, vigorous, and vibrant. We could see him meeting with the chairman."

> *The critical factor for success in Corporate America is to be attractive.*
> JAY GAINES, PRESIDENT, JAY GAINES & COMPANY

According to studies by behavioral scientists, 55 percent of the impression someone makes is due to his or her appearance. Voice counts for 38 percent and the substance of the conversation just 7 percent. And most recruiters agree that appearance is an excellent first screen for leadership presence. If you don't look the part, you'll rarely be allowed to demonstrate how well you communicate, how charismatic your personality is, or how brilliantly you think. And you need to look like the client so you won't clash with the corporate culture. "A critical factor for success in Corporate America is attractiveness," says Jay Gaines, president of New York–based Jay Gaines & Company. "Corporations hire in their own image or the image they like to see themselves. And if a candidate doesn't meet a minimum acceptable level, they won't be considered—no matter how smart or effective."

APPEARANCE HAS MANY DIMENSIONS

How you look involves more than just clothes: your height, weight, health, hair style, makeup, grooming, accessories, and even the condition of your cuticles all come under scrutiny. Appearance is something that every recruiter notices in exquisite detail—and analyzes carefully to determine your management style, credibility, people skills, and culture fit.

While their clients may protest that they want to recruit "fresh blood," an executive who "thinks outside the box," or a maverick who will "shake things up around here," the reality is that most organizations have very little tolerance for people who look and act differently from their current executives. If the company is recruiting a CEO, he or she needs to "fit" with its board of directors. Understanding the important symbolic power of appearance, recruiters are reluctant to recommend candidates who don't look, walk, and talk like the current board or executive committee.

POLISHING THE PACKAGE

The good news is that you can influence a recruiter's perception of you, and your viability as a candidate, by:

- understanding the client and how its executives dress and behave;
- showcasing attributes that you share with the client;
- leaving the impression that you look and act like an executive.

The creation of your package involves a lot more than clothes and physical appearance, but you won't get a chance to demonstrate the nonvisual components if the visual components don't meet expectations. Even if they are impressed by a candidate, recruiters must always keep their client's culture and executive "look" in mind when making judgments. Bonnie Crabtree, an Atlanta recruiter, once interviewed a top candidate for a CIO position at a young company that sponsored a bike tour for its employees, many of whom were amateur athletes. "Although he had an ideal background and solid references, he weighed 300 pounds and was short," says Crabtree. "His paper was great, and he was bright and witty, so I spent two hours interviewing him," says Crabtree. "But my client wouldn't see him. They felt he wouldn't fit in."

MAKING QUICK JUDGMENTS

According to Herman Smith, president of Toronto-based Herman Smith Executive Initiatives, "There are the candidates who look, sound, and feel terrific—we're lucky if we can find them. And then there are those who don't 'show' well. When these candidates meet the client, the immediate assumption is 'they can't do the job.'" Most recruiters say they will make a judgment about whether or not to recommend you to their client within five to ten seconds of seeing you and shaking your hand. They'll spend the remaining two hours gathering evidence to confirm their initial impression.

Jack Clarey, partner with Chicago-based Clarey & Andrews, recalls a search for the chief operating officer of a large professional services company. One of his top candidates was appropriately dressed and groomed—and wore a pinkie ring. "The board of directors just couldn't get over that pinkie ring," says Clarey. "Every time they debated the strengths and weaknesses of the finalists, the pinkie ring came up." Ultimately, the candidate lost out to another executive with less controversial accessories. "If I had to do it over again, I'd tell him to take off the ring for the client interview," says Clarey.

THE STANDARD "LOOK"

Every aspect of leadership presence is based on client custom and the nature of the executive position. And most companies expect executive recruiters to "send in" candidates who match a standard template. Although there are exceptions, corporate leaders are typically tall (six-plus feet for men, five-and-a-half-plus feet for women) and lean, with excellent posture.

"They all want an airline pilot," says Susan Bishop, president of New York search firm Bishop Partners. "A tall, trim man in his 40s who is in great shape and has a little gray hair seems to inspire confidence." Geography, industry, and customer base can tweak the basic look to some degree. And some companies in the computer, entertainment, and fashion industries actively seek candidates who offer casual or "high concept" looks and attire.

HEALTH AND FITNESS

Until the 1930s, business executives tended to be portly and sedentary. But over the last fifty years, as the image of business has grown increasingly vital and exciting and the health revolution has swept America, the ideal "look" for corporate executives has scaled down considerably. Most CEOs of Fortune 500 companies are slim and athletic, providing a model for business managers at all levels throughout corporate America.

Recruiters seek vital, alert candidates

To most clients, candidates who look like they exercise regularly appear healthier. While vitality and alertness typically decrease with age, every recruiter can cite examples of sixty-five-year-old executives who have more pep than thirty-year-olds. But avoid being too fit: "Men who do a lot of weight lifting tend to get that 'no-neck' look," says one recruiter. "Visible muscles—anywhere—are a turnoff."

Height can be a boost, all other factors being equal

"Tall people, both male and female, have a distinct advantage," says Kathleen Johnson, a partner with Houston-based Barton Associates, and height can often make up for other executive presence deficiencies. Shortness, however, is almost always viewed as a liability. Said another recruiter, "Short men typically have to work harder to counter a negative first impression than someone who's taller." For women, height is less important but is generally a positive addition. "But don't try to jack yourself up by wearing ultra-high-heeled shoes," warns one recruiter. "They look trashy in a business setting."

Body power needs to match brain power

The old maxim is true: a healthy body makes the mind appear healthier. "Today, individuals who are overweight, out of shape, and sluggish just don't seem as on the ball as fit executives," says Bonnie Crabtree, who has met many candidates who look the part on paper but not in person.

Susan Bishop recalls a candidate with a fantastic resume who turned out to be short and thin with a high-pitched voice and a weak handshake. Says Bishop, "His entire presentation went against everything on the resume."

Weight is a key issue

Most companies feel being overweight reflects poorly on a candidate's energy level and self-discipline. Kathleen Johnson recalls a candidate who was fifty pounds overweight. "He just didn't look like a dynamic, aggressive go-getter. The extra weight made him appear stooped and lumbering, not quick and agile. Although it had nothing to do with how well he could do the job, he simply didn't look like fresh blood, and our client asked that we look for other candidates."

Says Rich Hardison, a Dallas-based recruiter, "I presented a superior candidate who was a smart, tough, good strategist with top credentials and glowing references. But my client rejected him because he was 'old, fat and out of shape.' Sometimes I think appearance has become almost too important."

Companies recognize that rejecting candidates because they're overweight can create serious legal problems. Rarely will they tell anyone directly that obesity was an issue. One recruiter recalls presenting a female candidate with a superb reputation as a candidate for a division president position with a Fortune 100 company. "She was short, chunky, and very outspoken," he says. "Our client told us he liked her but wanted someone who was taller and less aggressive. They ended up hiring someone who looked the part—someone who looked, frankly, like an airline pilot."

BODY LANGUAGE

Most recruiters are skilled readers of body language and they closely observe visual cues to draw conclusions about candidates' intangible qualities. "If a candidate can't sit still or maintain eye contact, or if they have a distracting physical habit, it tells me they're not in control of themselves," says one recruiter. He recalls a situation in which a candidate couldn't keep her hands away from her shoulder-length hair. "She had a great background, but after watching her twirl hair strands for an hour, I decided she would make my client very uncomfortable."

Body language cues that make someone look like they belong in a senior management position include selecting a straight-backed chair, lowering yourself into it (as opposed to flopping), and positioning yourself on the front half of the seat. Recruiters say that crossing your legs is OK: men have the option of crossing them ankle over knee in a "figure 4" or knee over knee; women should always cross knee over knee. Keep your hands still or make occasional small gestures to underscore points. Look at the interviewer with a relaxed, alert facial expression, occasionally nodding or saying "unhunh."

CLOTHING: YOU ARE WHAT YOU WEAR

Tuned into external cues and highly sensitized to "what goes down" in their client's environment, recruiters are ruthless when it comes to assessing whether a candidate's attire is appropriate. A retained search firm has certain expectations for how executive candidates should look. Today, you need to "present" like a member of the upper middle class. This means average weight for your height and good grooming—no flakes, runs, or ripped cuticles.

Your appearance needs to telegraph the message that you could belong to any club, not just the Order of the Moose.

Men's attire

Recruiter Steve Darter of People Management Northeast once interviewed a candidate from the Southwest for a regional sales vice president position at a Connecticut-based insurance company. "He walked off the plane from Las Vegas in a shiny, tight suit, chest hair and gold chains in great evidence," says Darter. "If you didn't have to look at him, he was a terrific candidate."

Darter and other recruiters say that male candidates should come to interviews in a dark wool suit that fits and drapes well, a white, starched shirt with French cuffs and cuff links, high quality, well-polished black leather shoes with thin soles, and black hose long enough to cover your calves when you cross your legs.

You don't have to be on the cutting edge of fashion but you do have to be current, professional, and polished. If you want to move to the next level of management, dress like you belong there.
BERNADETTE PAWLIK, PARTNER,
PAWLIK-DORMAN PARTNERS

Female candidates have slightly more leeway, but not much

Well-made, classic clothing communicates stability and power. Preferred attire for an interview is a well-fitting dark suit, a light colored blouse, and dark pumps. Avoid shiny or clingy fabrics, extreme styles, short hemlines, or low necklines. And always wear long sleeves. A suit is preferable to a dress: jackets are a power symbol.

One recruiter interviewed a female health care executive for a position as second in command at a major health care products company. With a strong resume and experience in line and staff positions at a Fortune 50 company, she was ideally suited for the job. However, she didn't look the part. "It appeared like she had bought her suit at K-Mart—her whole appearance was just cheesy," says the recruiter. "If she had just worn a simple navy suit, she would have gotten that job."

Know your audience

Since the standards for apparel differ slightly from industry to industry, your interview wardrobe may need to shift depending on the recruiter's client. At the most formal companies, such as investment banks, appropriate clothing means a dark wool suit, starched white shirt with French cuffs and cuff links, Hermes-type tie, black knee-length socks, and black cap-toe six-eyelet laceup leather shoes. The parallel look for women is a navy skirt suit, silk blouse, designer silk scarf, black cap-toe pumps with two and one-half inch heels, and skin-colored hose.

For a technology company on the West Coast, the standards are much more casual. But whether you are interviewing at Microsoft or Goldman Sachs, with few exceptions, the more formally you dress, the more executive presence you have. Well aware that apparel has immense power to make them fit or not fit in a client environment, executives with presence are willing to set aside their own preferences to make a solid impression with a potential employer. They understand that the selection of clothing has much less to do with personal taste and much more to do with what others will think.

Apparel faux pas reported by recruiters have included polyester pantsuits, short-sleeved shirts, clothing made from shiny material, wide ties, and bow ties. One head-hunter who was eager to interview a candidate for a high-level position at a growing consumer products company was convinced his candidate would look the part. "He was phenomenal on paper and on the phone, and had glowing references," recalls the recruiter. "But when I met him at the airport, up walked a grungy looking guy in a wrinkled polyester suit, with an ill-fitting, short-sleeved shirt and a wide neon-colored tie. Technically, he was right on but his grooming was lacking in the extreme."

Most of the time, candidates who are inappropriately attired simply get rejected before they're passed along to a client. Says Bernadette Pawlik, "One of my candidates came to a formal interview in dress shoes, sports socks, and sweatshirt. I didn't write him up."

Dress the part

If your goal is to move from the front lines into a management position, be mindful of the wardrobe shift. Larry Tyler, who recruits exclusively in the health care industry, talks to many physicians in short-sleeved shirts and bow ties when recruiting hospital and health care system executives. "I tell them to wear long-sleeved shirts and ties for the client interview," says Tyler. "You can wear Dockers, short sleeves, and bow ties when you're practicing medicine, but administrators have to look and act the part. They can always go back to the bow ties once they get the job."

*As executives become classier, they can get fancier and
flashier. If a recruiter notices your clothes, you're probably
overdressed or inappropriately dressed. Your clothes should
focus attention on you—not the other way around.*
JACK CLAREY, PARTNER, CLAREY & ANDREWS

Beware of looking too nice

Recruiter Jack Clarey says that some executives—particularly those who came from a lower-middle-class
background—can overdo it once the money starts flow-
ing in. Says Clarey, "If we've noticed your clothes, you've
picked the wrong ones. Clothes should make you the
focus of attention—not the other way around." One
recruiter recalls interviewing a man who wore a gold ring
on every finger and had a lace handkerchief stuffed in his
pocket. "Even for the entertainment industry, this was a
little extreme," he says. Dennis Carey, managing partner
of Spencer Stuart's Philadelphia office, agrees that many
candidates disqualify themselves because they are too
slick. "In most companies, the products, strategy, and customers dictate what's considered acceptable as far as dress
is concerned."

Dick Cronin was recruiting a marketing executive for
a golf company. He interviewed the candidate en route to a
golf tournament, where both wore casual clothes. But
when the candidate showed up in casual dress for a meeting with the company's top executive at its corporate headquarters, all hell broke loose. Visibly annoyed, the CEO
told the candidate that it wasn't normal to come to an
interview without a suit. The candidate said, "This is who
I am—take it or leave it." And the company did. "When

you're interviewing with the president, dress like the president," advises Cronin.

Business casual

Norm Mitchell of A.T. Kearney Executive Search bemoans the ascendancy of business casual attire throughout corporate America. "It certainly affects someone's executive presence because many companies have brought business casual to a new low." Mitchell suggests that candidates wear formal business clothing to meet with recruiters, unless they work in a full-time business casual environment and are interviewing for a job in a full-time casual company. And client interviews? "Dress like you would for any other interview unless the client specifically instructs otherwise."

SHOES: THE WINDOW OF THE SOUL

Many recruiters are passionate about the subject of footwear. As one headhunter put it, "The shoes are the window of the soul." When you meet with a recruiter, beware: the shoes you wear may be even more important than your clothing.

The belt and shoes are what we look at more than anything else. Belts get worn out; don't like to see belts or shoes really abused. On women, don't like to see grown out or chipped nail polish or fake nails, lots of jewelry that clanks the table.
J. ROBERT CLARKE, PRINCIPAL, FURST GROUP/MPI

"I once interviewed a partner from a large accounting firm to be director of global tax for a manufacturing corporation," says Susan Bishop. "Her credentials were excellent.

Besides the Big Five experience, she had a master's degree in taxation and glowing references. But she strolled into the interview wearing a casual pantsuit and open-toed flat shoes. Those toenails! It looked like she thought we were getting together for coffee on Saturday morning."

The style of shoe you choose for your interview speaks volumes about your executive presence. While it's possible to disguise low-quality suits with scarves and other accessories, cheap shoes are impossible to mask. The designs are cruder, the leather is less resilient, and they often make noise. One recruiter recalls hearing her candidate's shoes squeak with every step he took.

The condition of your shoes is another recruiter cue. Shoes must be clean and well-shined and preferably thin-soled. One recruiter disqualified his top candidate when he showed up for the interview impeccably dressed but wearing "factory floor shoes"—wing tips with thick soles. Another Wall Street recruiter knocked a candidate back to waiting list status when he arrived for an interview wearing loafers instead of the requisite six-eyelet cap toe model.

Be sure to wear socks that cover your hairy legs. Recruiter Gerry Roche once interviewed the number two executive at a major chemical company for a position as CEO of a large packaging corporation. "This guy came into my Park Avenue office during the week in golf socks," says Roche. "Every time he crossed his legs, three inches of leg showed." But when Roche told him to get longer socks, "the candidate looked at me as if I were death incarnate." Ultimately, the candidate was selected for the position, but now wears only calf-length hose.

ACCESSORIES: SUBTLE, CLASSY, AND STATIONARY

Accessories are important tools for establishing and reinforcing your status and relative positioning. Ties, scarves, jewelry, handbags, briefcases, pens, and eyeglasses are just some of the items that recruiters make a point of observing during candidate assessments. The rules for accessories are clear cut: not too much and only the highest quality.

Jewelry for men should be limited to watch, wedding ring, and cuff links

Some men insist on wearing large class rings, but most recruiters advise against it because they look provincial. One recruiter recalls interviewing a male candidate for a position with an investment bank. "When I saw his gold bracelet and a big ring, I suspected he wasn't going to fly. And then he told me about his three divorces and holidays in Vegas. I rejected him purely on the basis of his looks and style."

Watches

Don't wear a clunky sports watch with a suit. A Chicago-based headhunter once recommended a highly qualified candidate for a position as a controller with a cable TV operations company. The client liked him but hated his watch, an oversized diving model with multiple hands and a plastic strap. "I could never hire someone who wears that kind of watch," said the client. "We're trying to raise money and that watch wouldn't pass muster with our Wall Street bankers."

Jewelry

Jewelry for women should be subtle and stationary. Avoid dangling earrings, clanking bracelets, rings with large colored stones, and anything oversized. Pearl earrings and necklaces cue recruiters that the candidate is "classy" and can be depended on to look tailored and professional.

Belts

Belts are another important symbol of a candidate's place in the pecking order. Paul Hawkinson, publisher of *The Fordyce Letter* and a former executive recruiter, recalls conducting a search in the early 1970s for a $300,000 director of advertising at a major oil company in Oklahoma City. After pinpointing a candidate in Minnesota and qualifying him over the phone, Hawkinson, relieved to find someone, was eagerly looking forward to meeting the man. "It's not that easy to interest executive talent in moving to Oklahoma City," he says. But the physical reality was stunningly off-target: "He had on a yellow cowboy suit and boots, a belt with a brass buckle that said "The Best," a handlebar mustache, and no front teeth. He was quite an eccentric," says Hawkinson. Other belt disasters reported by recruiters include a candidate wearing a large, Texas-shaped belt buckle; a man with a plastic belt from K-Mart that belied the Armani suit and Gucci loafers he wore; and a candidate who had tied a piece of laundry line around his waist because "my belt was at the cleaner's." Always wear a high-quality leather belt that matches your suit.

Even eyeglasses can make an impact

Ann Peckenpaugh of Schweichler Associates recalls a particularly difficult search in which her client continued to ask for "just one more person" every time she presented a top candidate. "Finally, the client hit it off with a candidate, and I realized why," says Peckenpaugh. "They both wore the same style of eyeglass frame. If candidates look like the client, they're more successful."

HAIR: CLEAN, WELL-STYLED, AND OFF THE FACE

If your hair is colored, be sure it's not time for a touch-up before your interview. For men in any industry except entertainment, retailing, and computers, facial hair—especially a beard—is a no-no. "It makes you look like a professor or a dock worker," according to one recruiter. Another says, "We're here to help our clients find qualified management talent, but we're also here to find them someone with whom they can be comfortable. Some clients tell us they can't trust anyone with facial hair. So we find them someone without it."

Women who have hair longer than shoulder length should cut it or arrange it off the shoulders and face, according to recruiters. "Long hair makes a woman seem less mature and diminishes her executive presence," says one recruiter. "Swinging hair is a distraction and although it's probably not meant to be a come-on, it can have that effect."

Some clients eliminate candidates who don't have any hair. When he first began conducting executive searches, Peter Crist, president of Chicago-based Crist Partners, introduced a well-qualified, bald candidate to a client. The client rejected the candidate, telling Crist, "I like his functional skills but . . . where's the hair?"

Other hair details noticed by finicky recruiters include bushy eyebrows that grow in one unbroken line across the forehead, hair on the front or back of the neck, and hair protruding from ears and nostrils. And there's nothing worse than a bad hairpiece, says recruiter Norm Mitchell.

POSTURE: WHAT MOTHER TOLD YOU

Your posture and bearing send strong messages about your self-confidence level and assertiveness. Recruiter Jack Clarey was conducting a search for a senior executive position at a large manufacturing company in the Midwest. One of his top candidates was an enormously qualified woman who was eliminated from contention because of her bad posture. "She was stooped over and looked like she had a hangover. Because of her qualifications, we presented her anyway, but she didn't have the command presence our client was seeking," says Clarey.

PERSONAL GROOMING: UNDER THE MICROSCOPE

While it's not necessary to look like Mel Gibson or Susan Sarandon, impeccable personal hygiene is a must. Bad breath, body odors, disheveled clothing, and unmanicured fingernails can kill a talented executive's candidacy faster than a bad reference.

Austin, Texas–based recruiter Ron Zingaro recalls conducting a search for a large, conservative Midwestern health care company. "The company wanted a senior R&D executive who could work closely with the top executive team as well as the company's research professionals. We found a candidate whose resume was right on the money, and I flew to San Francisco to meet him for breakfast," says Zingaro. "And then I saw him: disheveled clothes, shirt hanging open, and a large gold medallion. We eliminated him."

Says recruiter Todd Noebel, "If you want be to taken seriously as a professional, you need to dress like one. An executive represents his or her company to external and internal audiences, and a sloppy appearance or wrinkled clothing make people suspicious about the quality of their work and their attention to detail. You are under a microscope and need to be prepared."

Additional grooming no-nos include unbuttoned shirts, cologne overdoses, and poorly maintained teeth. "I once interviewed a candidate who had a large triangle of hairy skin protruding over his belt," says one recruiter. Others report being overwhelmed by obvious perfume, aftershave, and even breath mints. And Larry Tyler recently eliminated a candidate whose badly broken front teeth—and lack of explanation—distracted him during an interview. "I presented him to the client, but his broken teeth distracted them as well," says Tyler. "Clients can overcome a physical problem or handicap if it's God-given and untreatable, but they are pretty intolerant of physical problems that can be fixed," says one recruiter. "Dental problems are considered eminently repairable."

The Recruiter Scorecard: Appearance

ENHANCERS
Physical fitness
Impeccable grooming
Appropriate height/weight relationship
Conservative dress, matched to company
    environment
Dress one level up

DIMINISHERS

Cheap clothes
Poor posture
Too much cologne
Rumpled appearance
Chipped nail polish
Dangling earrings

AND NEVER . . .

Allow bare legs to show
Wear unpolished, run-down shoes
Have one eyebrow

7

HOW YOU
CONDUCT
YOURSELF

If your manner and bearing are faulty, you won't be recommended for an executive position.

The candidate and the recruiter were having lunch after a two-hour interview. "I'll have a New York strip steak, medium-rare, and make sure you move the onions away from the meat. I don't want any onions near the steak," said the candidate. Sure enough, the steak arrived, piled with cooked onions. "I thought I told you no onions!" barked the candidate to the flinching waitress. "Take it back and get me what I asked for!"

In another case, a candidate repeatedly asked the recruiter who her client was, what products they produced, and how long they had been in business—questions that were fully addressed in the position description and background materials she had sent him two weeks before the interview. "Why this guy flew 1,000 miles to talk to a mystery company is something I'll never figure out," says the recruiter, who scratched him off the list halfway through the interview.

Your resume and accomplishments may be exceptional. You can look like an airline pilot and talk like a TV anchor. But if your bearing and manners are faulty, you won't be recommended for an executive position.

To a recruiter, poise has three main components: self-confidence, preparation, and manners. Each of these factors figures heavily in a recruiter's evaluation of your leadership presence. It's impossible to transform your self-confidence level for an interview. But it's easy to diminish it, particularly if you forget you're on stage from the moment you enter the recruiter's eyesight until the moment you leave it.

> *You can tell in five minutes if it's going to be a go or a turnoff. People who look and act like leaders are relaxed, but alert, optimistic, willing to reach out to other people. They also maintain good eye contact and speak English properly.*
> BERT H. EARLY, FORMER PRESIDENT
> EARLY, COCHRAN & OLSON, LLC

Poised executives are highly sensitive to other people's feelings and reactions and are constantly conscious of how their own physical, emotional, and intellectual presence affects others. In a recruiting situation, they follow mother's best advice: they arrive on time, say please and thank you, treat others the way they would like to be treated, move their bodies with dignity and grace, and stand up straight.

SELF-CONFIDENCE

Every recruiter interviewed for this book mentioned self-confidence as the single most critical factor in a candidate's executive presence. But few were able to define what they meant by self-confidence. Some recruiters said it was the level of comfort and ease the candidate demonstrated in a stressful situation. Some said it was unflappability. Others said it was the candidate's ability to guide the discussion according to his or her agenda. Some additional self-confidence markers follow.

Small talk

Don't launch right into the job when you meet. At the executive level, you're expected to be able to handle several minutes of small talk when you first meet the recruiter. The best subjects for those who are trying to put each other at ease include the weather, your plane trip (or the recruiter's), or sports.

Directness

When responding to a question or making a comment, get to the point. Recruiter Helga Long says that some candidates are so eager to impress that they monopolize the conversation. "There has to be a give and take. If I want to know more, I'll ask more," says Long.

Don't overdo it

You are expected to be an active participant in the interview, not simply a head nodder. One-word answers suggest that you are uninterested, scared, or uppity. Steven Darter tells of a search in which the candidate, an unsmiling, heavyset man, walked into the interview room with a black Fedora pulled down over his eyes, his hands shoved in the pockets of a large black overcoat. "He looked like a Mafia don," says Darter. "When I asked him if he wanted to take his coat off, he said 'nope,' and it was like that for over an hour—him sitting there in his coat and hat, giving me one-syllable answers. I was afraid he was going to pull a gun on me."

Take focus

Taking focus means knowing you will be the subject of attention and planning for it in detail. Watch any top executive's internal gyroscope go to work as he approaches an unfamiliar situation. Before entering a meeting room, he'll know what to expect. He will make sure he's briefed about who he's meeting, the subject of discussion, the issues that will be raised, and the desirability of the potential outcomes. He'll pause slightly before entering, rather than rushing in headlong and confused. He'll make a beeline for the person to whom he'll be speaking and a warm smile will spread across his face. And he'll initiate the conversation by acknowledging the other person first. "Great to meet you, Sam—Fred Smith" or "Sam, I'm Fred Smith—nice to meet you."

> *You CAN work at it—dress well, extend your hand first, sit on the edge of your chair at attention, listen carefully and most important, watch how people with executive presence act.*
> MARY JANE RANGE, VICE PRESIDENT,
> BISHOP PARTNERS

BODY LANGUAGE

In control

Executives with presence are able to be still. They don't shift from foot to foot, pluck at their cuticles, or shake the leg they've crossed. Their movements are deliberate and controlled—no jerking or darting. And they don't appear flustered or "out of control" by blurting or interrupting. They don't dig around for writing implements, business cards, or plane tickets, nor do they call their office constantly. If they drop something, they pick it up gracefully, without scrambling. "When a candidate can't keep his eyes, hands, and mouth still, I get concerned," says Chip McCreary. Says recruiter Dennis Carey of Spencer Stuart, "Even if they don't feel in control, executives have to appear confident. The people below them need to believe there's someone at the control panel, or they'll bail."

Eye contact

Eye contact is a factor that virtually every recruiter surveyed mentioned. "It is such a critical part of executive presence and it always surprises me when a candidate won't look me in the eye," says Amanda Fox, a partner with Spencer Stuart. "Most top executives have it mastered, and it's essential to a candidate's poise." Among executives in the United States, the general rule is that the *speaker* in a conversation should find a way to break eye contact occasionally. However, the *listener* shows attention by spending relatively more time looking at the speaker. Candidates should make a point of providing the encouragement of eye attention, head nodding, and occasional "uh huhs" as the recruiter is speaking to send nonverbal messages about the depth of their understanding and attention.

> *Candidates with executive presence understand how to make appropriate eye contact, and they use their eyes to convey confidence and authority.*
> PETER DRUMMOND-HAY, MANAGING DIRECTOR,
> RUSSELL REYNOLDS ASSOCIATES

Handshake

Like most people, recruiters hate dead-fish handshakes and attribute them to lack of self-confidence, lack of interest, or bad manners. When we are looking for someone to run a major business and he or she offers only three inches of fingers, we sense immediately that this is not a take-charge person. Always be the first to extend your hand, grip firmly, and shake twice. Recruiters don't much like two-handed politician handshakes, and they take a dim view of any subsequent touching. And if you have clammy hands, be sure to dry them off before shaking.

> *When I'm looking for someone to run a major company and a candidate gives me three inches of fingers, I get a strong sense that this is not a take-charge person. A fish flop handshake is an immediate negative—it suggests a self-confidence problem.*
> SUSAN K. BISHOP, PRESIDENT, BISHOP PARTNERS

Comfort

Many recruiters say they closely observe how comfortable a candidate appears to be in the interview, considered by most people a highly stressful situation. What do they look for? Relaxed alertness, controlled intensity, and sense of ease in an unfamiliar setting. For many recruiters, a candidate's ease and comfort can compensate for a less-than-stellar resume or other "paper factors." Susan Bishop recalls conducting a courtesy interview with someone who had been recommended by a colleague for a CEO position at a technology company. "His resume just didn't look right. He was a corporate general counsel and had never had a line job or even worked in high-tech. But he ended up being one of my best candidates. He was tall, pleasant, and very much at ease during the interview. He sensed my concerns and asked me directly if it would be good idea to address some of them. And because he was able to communicate his career path and accomplishments so well, I realized he had the ability to do 90 percent of the job. My client loved him."

Bounce back

A candidate may be surprised or even startled by questions a recruiter may ask. But they shouldn't appear to be. "Some people can't hide their confusion or irritation," says Ron Zingaro. Often the recruiter is deliberately testing their reflexes. Recruiter Bruce Bastoky makes a point of asking candidates to discuss their biggest screw-up so he can assess their poise and credibility. "Executives with real poise have either thought that one through or can absorb it quickly and respond with an acceptable answer after a few seconds of thought. It's a wonderful opportunity for a candidate to show how he turned a sow's ear into a silk purse or how he demonstrates his problem solving capabilities." Candidates who tell Bastoky that they never had a screw-up get crossed off the list for good. "Never show surprise at questions you've been asked," says Brian Sullivan.

Happy face

Don't bother to meet with the recruiter unless you have some genuine curiosity about the position. Headhunters expect that candidates who give up valuable time to meet in person understand how the recruiting game works and are willing to play along. And they're dismissive of those who refuse to play by the rules. Headhunter Jack Clarey was recruiting a CFO for a publicly held technology company headquartered in a rural community. During the interview, Clarey's strongest candidate questioned him repeatedly about the difficulties of uprooting himself and his family from a large city and his ability to be happy in a rural location. "Needless to say, we rejected him," says Clarey.

> *Employers expect that every executive candidate has the right attitude as well as technical skills and aptitude. There just aren't that many senior level positions.*
> TODD NOEBEL, PRESIDENT,
> THE NOEBEL SEARCH GROUP

MANNERS

Courtesy

You're expected to act like a member of an exclusive private club, and your decorum should follow the basic principles of etiquette. If you concentrate on putting the recruiter at ease, you'll stop worrying about how you look and are less apt to lose control and blurt, drop, lunge, or appear nervous. Offer your own hand first. Say please and thank you. Make the recruiter, and any other people who might be involved in the interview, appear strong and knowledgeable to the outside world.

Executives with presence are courteous to people of all levels. No matter how high and mighty they are, they listen even if they have thirty things that are more important to think about.
DAYTON OGDEN, PRESIDENT, SPENCER STUART

Meals

"You can tell more about someone's poise and self-confidence from how they eat than you can in any other venue." Since poor table manners can threaten your candidacy, most recruiters recommend avoiding meals during the first interview. The dining table is cram-packed with land mines for deep-sixing your poise. Not only is it hard to talk and eat simultaneously; it's almost impossible to think and juggle menus, cutlery, drinks, waiters, and the other paraphernalia that goes along with food.

Gerry Roche recalls introducing an IBM marketing executive to a financial company that wanted to notch up the sophistication level of its marketing and sales efforts. "Back in the days when IBM was a real powerhouse, everyone wanted to emulate its marketing success," says Roche, who brought the candidate and the financial company's chairman together for lunch at a private club. The candidate, who was visibly nervous, told the maitre d' he wanted "Number two, and make it rare." After taking orders from Roche and the chairman, the maitre d' asked the candidate, in an acerbic tone, to confirm that he wanted number two, rare. "Not only rare, but very rare," shot back the candidate.

After exchanging sidelong glances with Roche, the chairman said, "You should know that number two—turbot—is a fish. If you eat it rare, you die." Chuckles Roche, "And he almost did."

Think about the details—who you're seeing, where you're going—and shape your behavior appropriately. And, says Roche, never order onion soup. Other recruiters are less avuncular. "A candidate's table manners are a window on his or her management style. Eating lunch with a candidate is the quickest way to smoke out a phony," says a Chicago-based recruiter.

Social graces

Executives with presence have a knack for making you feel you're the only person in the room, says recruiter Dale Winston. "It's no secret trick—it's a matter of focus and energy," she adds. Recruiters assume you will interact with their client the way you do with them, so avoid giving them the impression that you're doing them a favor by seeing them. Even if you're ambivalent, it's in your interest to act like you want to be there.

> *The best way to enhance your executive presence is to be humble. Ask good questions, do homework, keep your eyes open and your mouth shut, say please and thank you, take vacations, and make sure your home life is in good shape.*
> RUSSELL S. REYNOLDS JR., FOUNDER AND CHAIRMAN, RUSSELL REYNOLDS ASSOCIATES

Don't use the recruiter as a pass-through for expense reimbursements. Todd Noebel once took a candidate with strong credentials and referrals to lunch to discuss a tax executive position. The candidate unfortunately confirmed the stereotype. "He simply couldn't carry on a sociable conversation," says Noebel. "And he told me he was going to order dessert because it was on my expense account."

Recruiter Fred Siegel recalls conducting a search to find the president of an Oregon-based paper manufacturer. "On paper, my candidate was stellar: as executive vice president of a big manufacturing company, he had the operating and industry experience my client was seeking. I flew to the Midwest to meet him at 11 A.M. and though we met for only two hours, I was impressed by his communications skills, poise, and presence. I began to suspect something wasn't right when he sent me an expense report detailing charges for parking, lunch, and dinner. When he visited the client's plant, the reaction was "he's arrogant." After rescheduling his visit to the plant four times, he showed up dressed casually and was rude to middle managers and factory workers. Three references confirmed that although he was bright, he was rude and arrogant.

PREPARATION AND FOLLOWUP

Many executives fail to realize the responsibilities they accept once they agree to have their hat put in the ring. "Some candidates persist in believing that an invitation to meet with a recruiter is essentially a job offer, and their arrogance is usually insufferable," says one recruiter. Others claim they are interested in the position but refuse to provide background information or give anything but yes and no answers to questions. Others appear overeager and act like applicants—a sure way to impair executive presence.

Be prepared. Know about the company, the industry, and relevant trends. Walk into the interview like you're walking right into the boardroom.
DAVE PALMLUND, SENIOR PARTNER, LAI WORLDWIDE

Closely observe executives with presence and you'll note that they are in control of their feelings, actions, appearance, etc. They're also in control of information. Candidates for executive positions should learn a lesson from the executive who never enters a meeting room without reviewing a two-page briefing statement: don't meet with a recruiter until you've studied the position description, the company's annual report, and its promotional material thoroughly.

Recruiters are deeply unimpressed by candidates who ask for basic data or can't even remember the client's name. You can't ask intelligent questions if you don't know anything about the potential employer's industry, operations, and performance. A close look at the company's annual report and Web site is an absolute minimum before the interview. Don't ask questions that are plainly answered in these publications.

Candidates who arrive armed with notes and information on the client company impress me. I am further impressed when they bring a list of questions.
DALE WINSTON, CHAIRMAN AND CEO,
BATTALIA-WINSTON INTERNATIONAL

Most recruiters suggest planning a selected list of questions and issues you want to discuss before coming to the interview. It's not necessary to have them in writing before you meet, but it is essential to have an agenda. Merle Owens, a veteran executive recruiter based in Fort Worth, Texas, and other recruiters, expect candidates to take notes during the meeting. "A candidate doesn't need to write down everything that's discussed, but jotting some selected notes alerts me that he or she wants to record some new information for further reflection," says Owens.

Recruiters closely observe how candidates handle the end of the meeting. "If they're interested in the position, it's important that they ask me about next steps and when they will hear back from me again. The best candidates always want clarity about the process and the client's decision timetable. Those who simply shake hands and leave the room are either scared to death they made a bad impression or completely uninterested."

Recruiter Scorecard: Poise

ENHANCERS
Being prepared with questions, answers, evidence
Sense of ease
Appropriate eye contact
Punctuality
Good table manners
Relaxed control
High degree of comfort with yourself

DIMINISHERS
> Arrogance
> Lateness
> Evasiveness
> Self-absorption
> Defensiveness

AND NEVER . . .
> Ask if the job is big enough for someone like you
> Drink alcohol in a job interview lunch or dinner
> Run down your past or current employer
> Forget the name of the recruiter or his/her client

THE NEW JOB INTERVIEW, AND TEN WAYS TO BLOW IT

Candidates with superior credentials occasionally fall for the fallacy that showing up and answering questions is all that's required to get an offer. Even if the company is recruiting you, realize that you can easily blow yourself out of contention if you do the following.

1. **Act disinterested.** Headhunter Jack Clarey of Chicago-based recruiters Clarey & Andrews was recruiting a CFO for a publicly held technology company headquartered in a rural community. During the interview, Clarey's strongest candidate questioned him repeatedly about the difficulties of uprooting himself and his family from a large city and his ability to be happy in a rural location. "Needless to say, we rejected him," says Clarey. Don't bother to interview unless you have some

interest in the new position. The recruiter or company may have called you first, but you're expected to demonstrate curiosity and enthusiasm when you come to an interview.

2. **Don't do your homework.** You can't ask intelligent questions if you don't know anything about the potential employer's industry, operations, and performance. A close look at the company's annual report and Web site is an absolute minimum before the interview. Don't ask questions that are plainly answered in these publications.

3. **Talk too much.** An internal candidate for a top position at a major investment bank was an ideal match for the position specification, according to recruiter Jac Andre, partner with Ray & Berndtson. But he was automatically disqualified when he talked for more than an hour without making a single point. "He rambled on and on without answering my questions," says Andre. When responding to a question or making a comment, get to the point. Nothing demonstrates your lack of self-confidence more than endless commentary that goes nowhere.

4. **Talk too little.** You are expected to be an active participant in the interview, not simply a head nodder. One-word answers brand you as uninterested, scared, or uppity.

5. **Display bad manners.** Ann Peckenpaugh, a recruiter with Schweichler Associates, was convinced her candidate was a perfect fit for her client, a high-tech startup in Silicon Valley. "He was ideal on paper, and unlike many 'techies,' he was a good communicator on the phone," she says. But when

she met him in person over dinner, he horrified her by picking up his roast chicken dinner with two hands and eating it off the bone. Says Peckenpaugh, "We were waiting for him to growl."

6. **Run down your current (or past) employer.** Badmouthing your present boss is perhaps the ultimate interview offense. Recruiters and employers know that if you air dirty laundry about your current company, you're likely to be a malcontent in your next position as well. Even if you're convinced your boss is a felon, stick to your own accomplishments and the company's resulting performance when discussing your current situation.

7. **Take credit for things you didn't do.** While it's important to explain your role in accomplishing results, don't overstate your authority or responsibility. Anything you claim to have done will be thoroughly checked with current or former colleagues, customers, or bosses. And avoid saying "I" as much as possible. No one in a corporate environment does things single-handedly.

8. **Hide holes in your resumes.** Don't follow the example of the candidate who advised headhunter Chip McCreary, CEO of Austin-McGregor International, to avoid calling him at work because the voice-mail system was being changed. "Naturally, I called right away," says McCreary, "The receptionist told me he was no longer with the company." Periods of unemployment, dates, and degrees are all simple to detect. Address resume gaps or other potential concerns directly and have a

good explanation about why they made sense and what you learned from them.

9. **Show lack of confidence in the prospective employer.** Recruiter Steven Darter, president of People Management Northeast, once interviewed a candidate who spent an hour itemizing the recruiting company's problems. "He told me he could get it all turned around, but couldn't give me any specifics," says Darter. "We crossed him off the list the minute he left the room." It's OK to express concerns about some aspect of the potential employer's strategy, product line, or operations—particularly if you can suggest another approach that works better. But don't let the interview devolve into a critique session. Employers want managers who are excited by opportunities, not dismissive of past mistakes.

10. **Negotiate too early.** If you raise the issue of compensation, it's clear to recruiters and employers that your primary interest is money, not opportunity. Wait until they bring up the topic, and don't negotiate during the interview. Take a day to formulate your response.

8

WHAT
YOU SAY

What you say exposes how you think, how you relate to people, how you approach a problem, how you present a message, and how you deal with stress.

The candidate seemed like a solid fit for the COO position at the recruiter's client, a $2.1 billion financial services company. With a stellar background, an agreeable personality, and airline pilot looks that closely matched those of the company's CEO, the candidate was number one on the recruiter's short list. But when asked to summarize his most important accomplishments in his current position, "He just danced all over the place," the recruiter says. "I heard about the sales training program, the new computer system, the casual dress policy, the addition of international correspondent banking, the opening of four new branches, and on and on. But he couldn't relate any of them to the bottom line or tell me what impact they had on the organization's profitability or market position."

WHAT YOU REVEAL

Your resume, clothes, accessories, and haircut can make you look like a polished, successful executive. But when you open your mouth, you reveal a host of cues about your brainpower, people skills, poise, energy level, and passion—all factors that contribute to executive presence. Most recruiters say that what you say is the single most important factor in judging your worthiness for a position, because speech reveals far more than your ideas and judgments. It exposes how you think, how you relate to people, how you approach a problem, how you deal with tension, and how you present a message.

It used to be that executives stayed in their offices, and issued written memorandums that their secretaries disseminated to the steno pool or the factory floor. Not anymore. In today's instant-message culture, particularly in the United States, executives are expected to deliver most of their messages orally or electronically. Countless studies on organizational productivity have shown that employees' feelings about management's explanations of the company's future are one of the highest predictors of productivity and worker motivation. The better "connected" they feel to management's agenda, the more positive they become. It's no longer enough that people understand what's expected of them; they also need to accept it as well.

Today people no longer accept as a given that they should automatically do whatever it is that the company tells them to do. They have been brought up to think they have the right to understand why something is going to be done. They believe they have the right to judge the rightness of a policy, question leaders, and become personally involved in the decision-making process. Against this background, it is no wonder that senior executives are not only judged by but also totally reliant on communication skills to persuade, convince, and lead. Executives who can't connect successfully with a variety of audiences don't stand much of a chance for a senior management position.

Maybe you're one of the fortunate few who have been told you have superb communication skills. If so, you've probably had numerous recruiter encounters and are familiar with the advice in this chapter. But if you're like most executives, you're not sure your oral communications are as strong as they could be. Or worse, you're convinced your communication skills are superb and it's only a matter of time before everyone else realizes it.

A NOSE FOR FLUFF

Most recruiters talk to literally thousands of people every year and have highly sharpened diagnostic antennae and a unique talent for recognizing fluff, or worse, a vacuum. Recruiters are also skilled at pinpointing the communication shortfalls that can quickly torpedo your career as an executive.

Consider the candidate whose resume and pedigree appeared to be "spot on" for a position as senior vice president of marketing for one of America's largest commercial banks. Convinced she had the job in the bag, she spent two hours recounting the advertising campaigns she had launched during her tenure at a regional financial institution. "Every time I asked her a question about the bank's strategy or how she built the marketing function, she flipped back to those ad campaigns," says the recruiter who conducted the search. "The worst part was, she couldn't quantify the results the campaigns generated or even the costs versus the benefits."

On the other hand, most recruiters agree that strong communication skills can rescue a flailing candidate or strengthen the candidacy of a marginal executive. While recruiting a new chairman for a failed savings and loan, Dave Lauderback agreed to interview a candidate whose background was off the mark. Although the candidate had experience turning around floundering thrifts, his unorthodox education—he had attended chef school in Boston—concerned Lauderback. "Meeting him in person completely sold me on him," says Lauderback. "He exuded control and leadership and knew the players thoroughly. He talked in simplest terms about what had happened and outlined with razor-sharp precision what needed to be done. His communications skills got him the job—I saw in him the ability to succeed in a difficult situation."

YOU: THE STORY

Recruiters conduct extensive background research on candidates. Besides extracting data about your education, accomplishments, and executive presence from phone conversations and personal interviews with you, recruiters (or their assistants) confirm your academic degrees and employment history and explore what your former colleagues, clients, and bosses say about you through in-depth reference calls. But the primary service they provide their clients, besides pinpointing qualified candidates, is making sense of what all this information means. Faced with a sludge of objective evidence, subjective opinions, random perceptions, intuitions, and cues, the recruiter's professional challenge is to communicate your distinctive ability to manage the job at hand in a readable, digestible narrative.

> *Top candidates are able to draw parallels between their own experience and what the client needs. They're able to inte-grate—assess what the opportunity is and make a thoughtful evaluation of what they can bring to the company.*
> AMANDA C. FOX, PARTNER, SPENCER STUART

The culmination of the recruiter's service to the client is words on paper: a four- to six-page assessment written in a format that varies little from firm to firm. This assessment document describes the candidate's accomplishments, personality, and background and judges his or her suitability for the job laid out in the position description— the document that essentially drives the search process. Occasionally, the written assessment will be transmitted electronically to the client via the Internet, or in the case of some sophisticated firms, available to the client on a secure Web site. In an age of video and electronic communication, why do clients insist on written presentations? According to John T. Thompson, the Heidrick & Struggles vice chairman who has recruited more than seventy CEOs in his search career, "Clients like to see a written presentation because it maps it to their brain. It's probably because of our Western education, with its emphasis on the written word."

A BETTER STORY SELLS

Most headhunters relish the hustle and bustle of candidate interviews and think nothing of hopping on a transcontinental flight for a two-hour airport meeting with a candidate. But few look forward to putting words on paper—or keystrokes on computer. While there are certainly some who enjoy the painstaking, analytical process of weaving together a cohesive story from the evidence and opinions that constitute a candidate's file, many recruiters dictate segments of their candidate assessments for assembly at a later time by their assistants. Others simply edit drafts prepared by their assistants, some of whom have never met the candidate in person.

However, recruiters are savvy enough to know that a better story sells a candidate more quickly. And the candidate who can help them turn the loose tiles of evidence into a credible, compelling story is the candidate who stands the best chance of getting the job offer.

Your objective is to tell your professional story in such an effective, believable way that the recruiter simply transcribes your verbatim comments into a written format and passes it along to his or her client. How to do it? First, analyze the position specification to pinpoint the key intangibles sought by the client. Next, organize your story so it hits all the nails on the head. Finally, tell your story like a journalist, leading with strong summary statements and following up with evidence.

ANALYZE THE POSITION SPECIFICATION

Most position specifications provide the basic hard data on the position, reporting relationships, responsibilities, and client requirements. Although few explicitly state executive presence requirements, they provide important cues about the intangible qualities the company seeks.

For example:

Springfield International, Inc.
CONFIDENTIAL POSITION SPECIFICATION

POSITION

Senior Vice President of Corporate Communications and Investor Relations

Leadership presence cues: **New position for $1 billion company—means trouble. A company this size should have had an executive in this position as soon as it became public. Communication skills (obviously), poise, and intellect will be key to sell management on a strong communication program.**

COMPANY

Springfield International Inc. is a global semiconductor company with over 5,000 employees worldwide. Headquartered in Los Altos, CA, Springfield has operations in 16 countries, with strategic partnerships around the globe. Sales for 1998 exceeded $1 billion.

Opportunities: **Young public company with hot product; global business could grow dramatically if properly marketed.**

Leadership presence cues: **Language skills and overseas experience will be a plus. But "strategic partnerships around the globe" usually indicates internal communications issues. Los Altos is the heart of Silicon Valley; check about wearing business casual to interview. Management likely to be informal and collegial; little distinction between executives and workers. Experience in similar culture likely to be an important issue.**

REPORTING

This position reports directly to the senior vice president and chief financial officer. This position works directly with the Springfield senior management, including the president and chief executive officer, senior management of the operating groups, and other members of the management team in a collaborative fashion.

Leadership presence cues: **Company sees this position as a financial/shareholder relations job. Will need strong self-confidence and focus to broaden management's view of communications beyond mere financial reporting. Poise, appearance, and culture fit all key for operating at this level.**

EDUCATION   MBA; undergraduate degree in journalism, liberal arts or business

Leadership presence cues: **MBA probably essential; check management's educational background.**

REQUIREMENTS   10–15 years of corporate communications experience and a solid understanding of how communications plays a role in investor relations. Prior experience with high-level responsibilities and executive contacts is desired, in addition to demonstrated understanding of and success in communicating complex business issues and market dynamics.

This position requires strong analytical and communications skills; a successful track record in developing traditional and nontraditional internal communication programs; proven success in initiating and managing relationships with Wall Street and analysts; and experience with all types of media outlets, especially the national business, trade, and financial print media.

Leadership presence cues: **Executive contact means poise and appearance critical; intellect needed for complex business issues; communication skills an obvious must—internally and externally.**

RESPONSIBILITIES As the head of the corporate communications and investor relations functions, this professional is responsible for developing, reinforcing, and strengthening Springfield's positioning with both the internal and external constituencies.

The individual supports the business objectives of the company, specifically the global implementation of SAP, and develops appropriate strategies and materials in order to facilitate the delivery of key messages. Other responsibilities include the preparation of newsletters, videos, Town Hall presentations, e-mail, and related internal communications.

This professional defines Springfield's global corporate positioning message and determines appropriate strategies to deliver that message. The individual also works closely with the chief financial officer/controller to develop messages for quarterly SEC compliance materials.

Additional responsibilities for this position include maintaining a proactive relationship and serving as the primary liaison with the investment community and the media (financial, trade, and local) as well as responding to all media inquiries. This individual also prepares financial and other press releases, scripts and hosts conference calls, and develops analyst presentations.

Leadership presence cues: **Focus, intellect, poise, and communications skills all critical for**

dealing with projects and people, translating corporate-speak into everyday language, and juggling multiple internal and external audiences.

PERSONAL
CHARACTERISTICS The successful candidate should be a bright and articulate individual who is a strategic thinker with good listening and translation skills, possessing the ability to focus on the right message. This person should have exceptional personal communication skills, both oral and written. The position requires an individual who takes considerable initiative and has demonstrated the ability to operate as an individual contributor with little direct supervision. This individual possesses the strength of character to define and develop internal communications from a position of influence rather than authority. A strong work ethic with high standards for quality is imperative.

***Leadership presence cues:* intellect, communication skills, poise, focus, passion, culture fit.**

THE INTERVIEW SCRIPT

The executive recruiter or client is technically the one who controls the personal interview session. However, your ability to organize your story and leadership presence factors so they hit all the "hot buttons" will strengthen your candidacy dramatically. If you can walk into the interview carefully prepared to relate how your specific experience, strengths, and accomplishments can supply what the recruiter's client is seeking, you will provide exactly what the recruiter needs and demonstrate your communication skills, poise, intellect, focus, and interest in the job.

The best way to prepare is by creating a one-page interview script that aligns the company's needs with your strengths, expertise, and evidence.

Springfield International, Inc. Interview
Lloyd A. Jones
Senior Vice President of Corporate Communications and Investor
Relations Position
June 1, 1999

SPRINGFIELD REQUIREMENTS
10–15 yrs. of experience in:
* Corporate communications experience
* Investor relations
* Media relations
* Executive contacts
* Communicating complex business issues
* Internal/external communications
* Global strategies/positioning

JONES EXPERIENCE
12 years experience
* VP of marketing, Widget Telecom
* Handle all investor relations, media relations, marketing communications, executive communications
* Report to Widget CEO; matrix to CFO
* IPO; re-engineering communications plan
* Headed communications to all Widget audiences including JV partner in Asia and L. America
* Manage $5 million budget, staff of 10, outside agency
* Widget Jr. global launch
* Widget Jr. and Widget III; expansion to mainland China
* Alliances with Framco, De Viver, and Wong Ho

SPRINGFIELD REQUIREMENTS
* Successful track record

JONES ACHIEVEMENTS
* Recent marketing/communications strategy for
    * Core Internet Platform—$25 mm in sales

* Widget operating systems launch—profitable in 3 mo.
* Latin America market entry—beat projections
* Compensation program redesign—lost only 5% of staff
* Y2K–TBD
* 10 buy ratings from major sell-side analysts
* Stock price 15% compound annual growth
* 100+ media placements annually
* 50% more media citations than competitors
* Cover story—*Fortune*
* All collateral, product and package designs, annual reports 1990–98; Silver Anvil Award, 1996
* Revenues increased 18% annually; communications budget only 6% annually

---

SPRINGFIELD REQUIREMENTS
* Communication skills
* Focus
* Intellect
* Poise
* Appearance

EXECUTIVE PRESENCE TO-DO LIST
* Listen, challenge, be brief
* No SAP experience—discuss
* Questions:
  * Shift from geographic to product structure?
  * Corporate culture review?
  * Regulatory threats?
  * ABC's new Wadget IV—competitive positioning?
  * Sales force comp structure?

THINK—AND TALK—IN LEAD SENTENCES

A lead sentence is a proposition, a statement that summarizes a conclusion that you want your audience to adopt. And research has shown time and again that executives who punctuate their conversations with leads, backfilled with evidence and examples, are viewed as the strongest communicators. For example:

After becoming president of XYZ Inc., I restored the company's profitability.

As chief marketing officer for ABC three years ago, my challenge was to boost market share significantly in the widget industry.

Besides strengthening your communications, speaking in leads serves another valuable purpose: making the recruiter's life easier. Most recruiters prepare four- to six-page "writeups" summarizing why you should be considered for the job. These reports are sent to the client, on paper or electronically, and make the rounds of the board, executive committee, or the executive to whom your position reports. By providing recruiters with lead sentences, you enable them to compose your writeup more easily and accurately.

PROVIDE EVIDENCE

"It's surprising how some executives—particularly those who work in large companies—have no idea how to offer any tangible evidence of accomplishment," says John Martin, CEO of J3, a Dallas boutique recruiter. "I once interviewed a top international executive from Pepsico who had all the right tickets punched but couldn't tell me what he did for a living."

Before you issue forth with a lead sentence, be prepared to back it up with at least three pieces of hard data that demonstrate the impact on the business. Lead sentences are hollow without evidence to support them, and recruiters need the detail for their candidate writeups. Evidence is the physical reality that bolts a lead into place. For example:

Lead: When I became president of XYZ Inc., profitability, market share, and revenue growth were my top priorities.

Evidence: Here's how I approached it:

- Pinpointed our current situation. Had accounting provide a three-year P&L statement for each operating company, along with a competitor profile and projections of our sales volume versus the competition.
- Confirmed our high market share numbers through an independent market research survey. Surprise—in each case, actual share was 10 to 15 percentage points lower than what we initially thought.
- After several brainstorming sessions with the marketing team, we decided the only way we could maintain our revenue growth and increase market share was through acquisition.
- Since 1996, when we acquired ABC, my priority has been getting the two companies to work hand-in-glove to build market share and customer loyalty.
- It's been a remarkable success story: last year, revenues grew 25 percent and profits jumped 38 percent. For the first time, we had the lead position in the widget industry, and our stock price has gone through the roof.

Recruiter Scorecard: What You Say

ENHANCERS
Presenting a story
Relating your experience to client's needs
Using lead sentences and organized evidence

DIMINISHERS
Rambling
Weak or little evidence
Inability to quantify

AND NEVER . . .
Come to an interview unprepared
Badmouth your current employer

9

THE FIFTEEN QUESTIONS RECRUITERS ASK MOST

Never wing it.
JOHN R. BERRY, PARTNER AND DIRECTOR,
HEIDRICK & STRUGGLES

Every recruiting assignment involves unique specifications and requirements. However, most recruiters assess the candidate's leadership presence during the personal interview. Assuming that past behavior is the best predictor of future performance, recruiters use behavior-based questions heavily to extract evidence of the traits and skills needed in the position.

In addition to studying the client's position specification, Web site, and background and aligning your material appropriately, as explained in Chapters 7 and 8, always:

- come prepared with vignettes—examples of projects, plans, accomplishments, mistakes corrected, and results to cite as evidence;
- prepare at least five solid questions for the recruiter;
- polish your responses to the fifteen questions that every recruiter will ask—or expect you to address:

1.   What do you like/dislike most about your current position?

The recruiter is looking for skills and experience you will transfer from your current position to the new position as well as which new experiences, challenges, or skills you are seeking

To answer this question successfully, you must talk about why your current job is interesting, what specific aspects of it you find stimulating, and why and what the "missing component" is—what you wish you could be doing, in addition to your current responsibilities. For example, you might say, "As VP of marketing, I've been responsible for product development, market research, strategic positioning, and advertising. After building the marketing effort from the ground up three years ago, I'm happy to report a 35 percent increase in revenues due to new products and cross-branding. Our team works very effectively with our operations and R&D professionals and we've established a reputation as one of the top marketing shops in the widget industry. What I'm looking for is a chance to help a company expand globally. We've had some limited efforts in Mexico and Canada, but management's heart isn't in the international marketplace, although it's amazingly profitable."

Avoid what you dislike altogether. Remember how important it is to be positive: criticizing your current or prior employer is a warning flag. The best way to couch dislikes is to say your current employer is great but you are looking for more responsibility and the chance to make a greater contribution. You might say, "I've been happy and successful at Widget, but I was intrigued with the ABC position because it could allow me to have a wider span of control and contribute in different areas."

2. What are the most challenging aspects of your current position and how do you approach them?

The recruiter isn't looking for a list of complaints about what you find difficult. He or she wants to know how you have handled the opportunities of the position. You should address why your position is critical in helping your company make money, save money, or save time. You also need to be prepared to discuss the strategies or tactics you have implemented to make money, save money, or save time, including procedures you implemented and bottom-line results you achieved.

Another point to address is how your current position has helped you grow as a professional. You might say, "I've had a challenging time keeping our sales force consistently motivated. Here's what has worked for us recently . . ."

3. What are the most important things you will bring to a new position?

This is an opportunity to mention the items you selected when you compared the position specification with your own skills, experience, and interests. The idea is to provide a selected group of high points, with evidence and illustrations, rather than a laundry list of claims. If the position specification mandates the ability to perform in an environment where marketing activities will have a measurable impact on firm-wide financial performance, be sure to describe the marketing campaign you recently launched and its strong, positive impact on your company's revenues.

If the position specification mentions the importance of planning and consensus management, one of your comments might be, "I am a strong believer in planning a project or initiative and gaining buy-in from the key groups who will be affected by the program before starting it. For example, . . ." Be sure to mention at least one people-related skill you have, such as the ability to manage teams, or your experience with 360° feedback programs. In addition, since virtually all executive positions require reliability, perseverance, and good communication skills, mention that these three attributes are an important part of your philosophy of management, and provide an example that demonstrates your capabilities.

4. Why are you considering making a change at this time?

Don't say, "You called me—why do you think I should change?" Your answer must address why you want to join the new company, not why you want to leave your current organization. If you have reviewed the position specification and pinpointed the company's strengths and opportunities, now is the time to mention them. Don't forget to mention how your experience and success have prepared you well to take on the new challenge.

You might say, "I've always been interested in exploring how I could work with a major international consulting firm and serve clients representing a broad mix of the best companies in business today. I share ABC's professional philosophy of providing successful, cutting-edge solutions, and I'm convinced that a strong marketing unit can enhance the firm's world class image. The opportunity to serve as ABC's marketing vice president would allow me to draw on my expertise and experience in professional services marketing and enable me to expand my strategic and management capabilities."

Career blockage is always an acceptable reason as well. You can say, "I don't see much upward mobility because my boss was just promoted to COO and there's a logjam at the EVP level."

5. What is it about you that would get my client most excited about considering you as an executive for their company?

This is your opportunity to give your own PR speech. If you have analyzed the position specification carefully and prepared your interview script, this should be a piece of cake. Simply restate the must-haves from the position specification, preceded by, "I have solid experience . . ." or "I've proven . . ." For example:

- "I've had ten to fifteen years of progressively responsible marketing or communications experience, with a significant portion at the management level . . ."
- "My experience at Widget demonstrates that I'm a self-starter and a take-charge leader who is hard-working, no-nonsense, bright, and well-grounded."

- "I've demonstrated the ability to manage national marketing programs and provide counsel to partners and managers on developing tactical marketing programs to reach target audiences."
- "I've built and managed a regional marketing team providing the energy, drive, and focus to reach the firm's expectations for profitability within the region."

Don't forget to give the recruiter ammunition—examples and evidence—to fight for you. Finish by saying, "I'm also excited by the possibility of working closely with a team of committed professionals to help ABC attain its strategic goals."

6.   How do your responsibilities and accomplishments relate to your career objectives?

The recruiter wants to know your career plan, along with an assessment of how far you've come, what you have left to accomplish, and what you're doing about it. The drill for answering is:

First, describe your career objectives in a general way. "My goal is to lead a new technology company to a significant position in the personal computing market."

Second, dissect your approach and discuss what you've done so far. "I've always believed that three key areas drive the success of any new venture: engineering, finance, and marketing. I got the basics out of the way early on, with an electrical engineering degree from Cal Tech and an MBA from Stanford. Then I spent four years in product development at Microsoft, where I learned about branding, add-on marketing, and direct sales. Michael Jones recruited me to head up Widget's marketing operations in 1995."

Third, discuss your current plans. "We have an exciting marketing effort underway, but I don't want to stay in a marketing role too much longer. Now that I've covered all three bases, I feel it's time to move back to general management."

7. What are your most important accomplishments?

This is another opportunity to align your experience with the position specification. Select at least three examples of projects or programs and tell how they helped the company make money, save money, or save time. Ideally, these are projects that you initiated or played a major role in. Relate your examples to the capabilities desired. The more quantitative information you can provide, the better. Where possible, summarize your results in dollars increased or saved, market share increased, number of new customers, employees, etc. Are your programs/projects still in use with customers or within the company?

If the position specification stipulates a more intangible skill, such as "an ability to work well in a highly matrixed organization where change occurs frequently," you might discuss the challenges of designing a brand awareness campaign in your organization's matrixed structure or cite some of the changes that took place while you were there.

8. What are you seeking in your next career move?

Don't say "more money"! You need to make three key points: you want to continue growing as a professional; you seek the opportunity to make a significant contribution to an organization that can benefit from your unique strengths and experiences; you are committed to expanding your capabilities and taking on a broader range of challenges.

9. Describe a problem or crisis situation you faced and how you handled it.

Recruiters like this question for three reasons: it provides evidence on how you actually solved a difficult problem; it reveals your general approach to handling challenging situations; and it allows them to see your leadership presence in action when you answer with aplomb and finesse a question that makes most people squirm.

The key is to select two or three problems or crises and rehearse your response ahead of time—not get caught on the spot and start scrambling around for problems to recount. To enhance your credibility and show how you handled a no-win situation by mitigating disaster or containing fallout, pick at least one problem that didn't have a happy ending.

First, provide a nutshell description of the problem. *Second,* describe your mission. *Third,* discuss your analytical approach. *Fourth,* explain how you solved the problem.

10. Describe a difficult business decision you had to make. What did you learn?

Recruiters ask this question to determine how you define "difficult," how you actually handled the situation, and whether you drew any knowledge from it that could be applied to the job they're trying to fill. You must have one or two stories prepared for this question where the situation was tough and allowed you to show yourself in a good light.

One story should address a business risk you took, such as expanding to Europe without a clear read on the market.

Another example should focus on terminating a person or a group of people for a strategic reason that ultimately benefited the company. Be sure to express your concern for their lives and families, but emphasize that once you had analyzed the problem and selected an approach, you acted quickly and professionally with the best interest of the company at heart.

11. Tell me about a major project you worked on. Tell me about a method/program idea you have developed that has had a major impact on the company. Tell me about a project in which you demonstrated leadership and/or mentoring skills and describe how you demonstrated those skills.

You can be sure you'll be asked at least one of these questions, and probably two of them, during your interview. Recruiters use them to gather evidence that you actually did the things you have claimed to do on your resume. They also like to tell their clients in detail about your strategic approach, your management style, and how you assembled resources to get the job done.

Be sure to have at least two projects dissected and prepared for these questions. Choose projects that highlight one or more of the required or desired attributes listed in the position specification.

12. What legacy will you leave? How will they remember you?

Don't just sit there and say "I don't know." The recruiter is looking for an "obituary," a high level summary of your major accomplishments. It's important to begin your response with a lead sentence and substantiate it with evidence. For instance, "I put sales forecasting, budgeting, and an incentive compensation system in place five years ago. It's generated $250 million in sales and we're still using it."

13. "If I were talking to your boss, what would he or she say?"

A simple "Great" will not do. First, it's highly unlikely the recruiter will call your boss. The recruiter is looking for two things: your ability to present a balanced perspective of yourself, and your views on how you deal with authority figures. It's critical for a senior manager to be able to discuss his or her strengths and weaknesses using specific examples and stories. More important, this question provides a wonderful opening for discussing how you work with other people, the nature of your relationships, your critical role on the executive team, and the specific value you bring to the team.

14. Describe one of the best ideas you have sold to the CEO, board, etc. What was your approach to convincing them it was a worthy idea?

One of the key attributes of leadership presence is the ability to persuade others to accept a certain point of view. The art of influence entails handling other people's emotions, and star performers have a distinctive ability to send emotional signals and communicate powerfully. Executives who are strong influencers are highly conscious of how they go about winning people over and can describe their tactics. To answer this question effectively you must do the following:

First, show how you pinpointed a problem or opportunity. *Second,* show how you put together a solution. *Third,* show how you presented the information to get management's buy-in. *Fourth,* describe the result and the impact.

15. Give me an example of a situation in which you failed or had less-than-desired results.

Recruiters find the way candidates discuss weaknesses or failures to be hugely telling. Candidates who are able to discuss how they handled mistakes or bad decisions demonstrate that they:

- are willing to take a risk and experience setbacks;
- have been educated about a problem at another company's expense—most of the best executives have advanced their careers by learning from their experiences;
- accept responsibility for their own human failings;
- are not stymied by self-created problems;
- have the perseverance to turn things around;
- are balanced in their approach—they know some things will go wrong and they can deal with it.

Senior executive positions require a mature attitude about strengths and weaknesses. Candidates who are unwilling to admit that they made an error get flustered when I ask them what they have learned from their mistakes. Those who are confident will say, "That's a good question."
RON ZINGARO, PRESIDENT, ZINGARO AND COMPANY

Before talking to a recruiter, make sure you have two weakness/failure examples prepared and rehearsed. However, don't go overboard. It's important to pick a situation that you ultimately "got right," not one that became an unmitigated disaster. Answering by using a three-part formula is most effective.

First, state a misapprehension or misconception you held in the past. Describe the wakeup call that made you realize you were wrong. *Second,* discuss how you changed and what the results were. *Third,* assess the aftermath of the problem.

Depending on how the conversation flows, you might even preempt the question about your mistakes, which will inevitably be asked, by offering an example.

Avoid picking problem situations that have to do with personal issues between people, personnel issues, or anything illegal.

QUESTIONS THAT POSITION YOU AS A STRONG CANDIDATE

The questions you ask the recruiter demonstrate your executive presence just as much as your responses to his or her questions. Always have three to four strategic questions on the client's business, industry, threats and opportunities, or strategy. Make sure the questions haven't been addressed in the annual report, 10-K, or other published information on the company. Some examples might include:

How does ABC & Co. plan to position itself around DEF's new Internet product line?

Where does ABC intend to take its overseas telecom business once China lowers its trade barriers?

What does ABC hope to accomplish by its acquisition of Utah Widget Works?

In addition, don't hesitate to ask the recruiter several questions to gain more insight into the position. Strong possibilities include:

What's the potential career path for this position?

In other words, what happens if I do a good job? Do I get a promotion, a raise, a transfer, or what? The answer to this question will tell you a lot about how the company views your position. Most recruiters realize that this is a key concern of candidates, particularly those who have to be pried from their current situation. If the recruiter is unable to answer in a credible way, it almost always means the client doesn't know or doesn't care. If they haven't thought ahead enough to decide where they might put you next, it's a sure bet they view your position as a staff role—a support function only. Or they might see you as a stop-gap solution to a problem that will be fixed, possibly eliminating your job. Alternatively, they might simply be too disorganized to think that far ahead.

How does this position reflect the organization's strategic goals?

The recruiter should be able to summarize the company's goals and relate the position to it. Feel free to probe whether management views the position as integral to its strategy or "nice to have," why the company is looking outside instead of promoting from within, as well as who in the organization is convinced of the need and importance of the position.

What is your client trying to accomplish through this position?

A strategic way of asking, "What are their expectations for my performance, and how will I be measured?"

What are the major issues of this company's key constituencies?

A friendly way of finding out about the big problems the company has.

What do you feel someone with my background and experience brings to this position?

This is a fancy way of asking how your background and capabilities match the client's needs. It's perfectly acceptable to ask this to get a read on how you did at the end of the personal interview. Don't expect an entirely candid response. The recruiter needs some time to reflect on what he or she has heard and compare it with other candidates in the pipeline. If you're the number one choice or there are no other candidates in the pipeline, expect to hear highly positive feedback and maybe a little selling.

10

HOW YOU
SAY IT

*How you say it is often more important than what you say.
Recruiters observe many different aspects of how you
communicate.*

A promising young financial executive appeared to be an
excellent candidate for a chief financial officer position at a
growing consumer package goods corporation. But poor
grammar and malaprops deep-sixed his all-but-certain candidacy. "He kept telling me about assignments his board
had given to 'the CFO and I' and how "fortuitous" he was
to have been promoted," said the recruiter. "I shudder to
think that I nearly presented this guy without an interview.
My client has no patience whatsoever for lapses in English."

In another search, the candidate for a marketing executive job was a well-respected brand manager at a major
pharmaceutical corporation. When the recruiter asked her
to discuss two of her recent successes, she launched into a

fifteen-minute discourse on the company's new and improved beta blocker, complete with biochemical jargon, research results, and detailed accounts of the laboratory analyses. "She just couldn't get to the point," says the recruiter. "I think she thought I was a physician who wanted to test the drug on one of my patients." Although her product knowledge and technical marketing capabilities were clearly excellent, she couldn't shift her communication style to match the audience at hand.

THE ONLY WEAPONS

Communication skills are vital to the senior executive. They are the only weapons he or she has to engage the organization on terms that are likely to make it the most effective and productive over the long haul. But it doesn't matter how smart you are, how right you are, or how much you know. If the rest of your organization doesn't understand what you think or think they do understand but have something different in mind, you will fail as a leader.

How you communicate is as important—if not more important—than what you say. Many executives have learned the hard way that the content of your message will disappear quickly behind your grammatical lapses, jargon, homeboy accent, and inability to get to the point. That's not to say that inarticulate, monosyllabic, or grammatically challenged executives can't succeed. But it makes the job more difficult and the odds against success more substantial.

For recruiters, and for many of the boards that ultimately hire top executives, how you say something is often more important than what you say. And they observe many different factors.

Succinctness

"I've talked to candidates who lean back in their chair and spin story after unrelated story—conversational rice cakes," says Todd Noebel of The Noebel Search Group. "There's lots of volume but not much nutrition: the point isn't clear, the story line bounces around, and once you've gone home and digested the words, you realize nothing's been said." Recruiters detest being confused by double talk or talked to like a child, and long-winded speeches or five-minute responses to questions that deserve a five-word answer impress few. Get to the point quickly using simple words and declarative sentences. Be sure to answer the recruiter's question directly, but avoid being too abrupt. "We once flew halfway across the country to meet a candidate who was great on paper, only to hear him answer 'Yup' and 'Nope' to our questions," says Pat Campbell of The Onstott Group. "His one-line answers made him seem like an applicant."

Context

Executives who are good communicators don't give simple yes or no answers, particularly when they are trying to impress a recruiter. Instead, they respond to questions with a framework for an answer, demonstrating their strategic thinking ability and their capacity for generalization, a sure sign of someone with brainpower. If the recruiter asks you how your boss would rate your performance, don't simply respond "Very good." Demonstrate your intellectual and communication skills by saying, "My boss would judge my performance on three criteria: profitability, employee turnover, and sales growth. Here's how I made an impact in each of these areas . . ." If the recruiter asks you to describe something you did that made a significant impact on your company, don't say, "I sold more business last year." Place your answers in context by saying, "Under my direction, the marketing department has evolved from an in-house print shop to a comprehensive business development operation that generated more than $16 million in sales. Here's how we made the change . . ." Always try to relate your answers to the company's strategies and results, but be sure you have good evidence to put forth.

Bullet talk

Recruiters look for the ability to explain a complicated concept simply and coherently. "The ability to explain a complex issue in simple language is something we always observe in personal interviews," says Tom Neff, president of Spencer Stuart, one of the world's top recruiters. Executives with presence don't simply speak clearly. The best communicators speak in bullet points—short phrases of sixteen words or fewer. They also use easily understood metaphors or graphic images to get their point across. "In their role as the company's top spokespeople, senior executives need to make themselves understood to multiple internal and external audiences," says Brian Sullivan of Sullivan & Co. "They need to think in pictures and be able to summarize their vision in a short paragraph." And when they ask questions, they do it with simplicity and ease. "Candidates who ask me arduous questions so convoluted that only a specialist would understand don't have the gift of executive communication," says Bill Matthews of Heidrick & Struggles.

*Lots of big shots have short attention spans. If you
haven't made your point in sixty seconds, they're looking
out the window.*
DAYTON OGDEN, PRESIDENT, SPENCER STUART

Push back

Don't feel you have to keep the recruiter happy for two
hours. Recruiters don't like passive Pollyannas who sit,
smile, and nod at everything they're told. Remember, the
interview is a two-way conversation and you, as a candidate, are expected to hold up your side as well. Sometimes
this means challenging the recruiter on the company's
strategy, questioning why the company does things a certain way, or seeking more detail about the company or the
job. Says headhunter Gerry Roche, "Don't lick boots. I
want to know there's a piece of meat in front of me."

Command of conversation

Recruiters are split on the issue of who runs the interview. Many feel that they should manage the agenda and
lead the questioning. Others say they appreciate it when
the candidate takes the bit in his or her teeth. Whichever
option the recruiter prefers, it's important that you take an
active role in the conversation and query the recruiter
about the job and the client. If you don't, you'll come
across as uninterested or desperate for a new job.
Remember that headhunters prefer to recruit executives
who are happily employed elsewhere. Even if you're
secretly looking for a new job, you need to make it clear
that you are being extremely deliberate in your decision-
making process or else you'll be perceived as an applicant.
Have a list of questions prepared from your reading of the

company materials and any other research you've done, ask questions, and offer suggestions. A gambit that many recruiters recognize but find impressive nonetheless is asking whether the client company has tried a tactic you used successfully at your own company. You can use this lead-in to discuss your own success.

> *The ability to lead requires gaining and holding attention. It*
> *means active, intense listening. I observe how candidates*
> *process what they hear; how they ask questions, rephrase;*
> *probe, guide and put information into perspective.*
> STEVEN DARTER, PRESIDENT,
> PEOPLE MANAGEMENT NORTHEAST

Listening actively

Many candidates, like the one described at the start of this chapter, believe the interview is a one-way forum for presenting their ideas, skills, and accomplishments. In reality, it's a two-way, highly choreographed dance where both parties gain some content information—and a lot of intangible information.

> *Demonstrate your listening skills by feeding back a synopsis*
> *and dead-on response to the recruiter's question. Incorporate*
> *the colloquialisms used by the recruiter in your response.*
> JIM MCSHERRY, SENIOR VICE PRESIDENT AND GEN-
> ERAL MANAGER, BATTALIA-WINSTON INTERNATIONAL

A common mistake candidates make is asking questions that the recruiter answered earlier in the interview. "This tells me they're not really listening to what I'm saying but thinking about how they can impress me with their next question," says Helga Long, managing partner of Horton International. She recalls a candidate who asked the same question over and over. "He was so nervous he wasn't even listening to himself," she says. Recruiters will often test candidates to determine whether they are paying attention by repeating an important fact or piece of information later in the conversation, using different numbers, names, etc. "I'm always a little suspicious of the ones who just let it go by," says one recruiter. "It tells me they don't care enough to make a point of it or the information simply didn't register. I worry that similar information won't register once they're in the job."

The evil I

It's impossible to avoid referring to yourself in the first person singular occasionally, but steer clear of beginning too many sentences with "I." It brands you as an egocentric loner who doesn't much like working in teams. Substitute "we" or "our team" as much as possible. A caveat: don't be too slick.

Recruiters easily detect "professional candidates," executives well trained by outplacement firms or career counselors to run the interview according to a set agenda and avoid all telltale signs of arrogance. "Nothing you ask seems to throw them—they're too smooth," says Chip McCreary of Austin-McGregor International. "They tend to talk about confidence and empathy, and they overuse 'we.' Sometimes you just have to say 'I.'"

Client-speak

Recruiters are impressed when candidates can catalog their accomplishments using the client's language and buzzwords. For example, a candidate for an executive position at IBM would be well served to talk about how he or she "mobilized to execute" and "focused to win."

Rhetorical questions

Although every recruiter comes to a candidate interview prepared to ask a list of standard questions as well as specific questions, they are delighted when the candidate raises some of the questions that they would ordinarily ask, particularly about gaps or other unorthodox career changes. For example:

> Why would someone with my background and experience be interested in this position? Because . . .

> What were the circumstances of my leaving ABC for XYZ? First, . . .

> How often did the senior management team take my advice? Almost always . . .

Rhetorical questions can also be used to position yourself as knowledgeable about an industry, company, or strategic decision. For example:

> Why did Widget decide to ride the coattails of Magnosoft in entering the global software market? Because . . .

> How does Jones & Smith compete against industry giants like Andersen Consulting and Bain? Three ways . . .

Framers

Framers are introductory sentences that cue the recruiter that you are about to say something noteworthy or meaningful. A device used routinely by politicians and public speakers, framers are also a hallmark of senior executives and management consultants, who work closely with senior executives. They not only draw attention to the statement that follows, but also strengthen it. Some of the most widely used framers include:

> Here's what my recommendation is. (Note: This formulation sounds much stronger than "I recommend.")

> Let me tell you about . . .

> I'd like to share a story about . . .

> I'm sure you must have some concerns about . . .

Volume

Several recruiters mentioned that soft-spoken candidates are at a distinct disadvantage because it's generally assumed that executives have powerful, dynamic voices. While no one wants to listen to a bellower, variety is the spice of life and the most effective communicators modulate the volume of their voice to suit their audience and the content of what they are saying. Without feeling and passion, or at least of the illusion of it, communication is ineffective and certainly unmemorable.

Vocabulary power

Nothing makes an executive look dumber than using the same words over and over or, even worse, using the wrong word. Richard Brinsley Sheridan's Mrs. Malaprop, the character who said, "If I reprehend anything in this world . . . she is having a historical fit," has many legacies in the corporate world, according to recruiters. While it's impossible to develop a broad vocabulary overnight, or even for a job interview that's scheduled next week, recognize that the vocabulary of those at the top of the business caste system is almost always broader and more colorful than that of those lower down.

Building a strong vocabulary is the result of reading widely in a variety of fields, including fiction and literature—generally the best writing there is. A diet of business books, spy novels, and the sports page won't do much for your vocabulary. Read a national newspaper like *The New York Times* and a business newspaper like *The Wall Street Journal* daily. Be sure to read the editorial pages, where opposing viewpoints are presented with style and intensity.

Accent

With few exceptions, headhunters agree that sounding like a good old boy or girl is not an effective way to get yourself recruited. A light Southern drawl may seem charming, but a heavy New York, New England, or Midwestern speech pattern can be a real turnoff to recruiters, particularly when they're looking for a CEO or executive whose job requires extensive personal contact and visibility. In most organizations, the doors to the executive suite swing open faster to those who observe a strict code of behavior, which includes accent-free speech. While there are exceptions to this rule, particularly for technical specialists like accountants or engineers, the most impressive executives talk like TV news anchors.

Pitch

The tone at which you speak is, strictly speaking, beyond your control. However, many candidates find that tension or nervousness makes the pitch of their voice rise, or even squeak. Some candidates, particularly women from the South, tend to end declarative sentences with a rising inflection, making their comments sound like questions. To a recruiter, this makes a candidate appear doubtful and submissive. Keep your voice in its lowest register, avoid rising inflections, and do some stress-release isometric exercises immediately before meeting the recruiter if you feel yourself becoming tense.

Cadence

Research shows that the optimal speaking speed for audience attentiveness and understanding is 175 words per minute. But with few exceptions, the higher up the chain of command, the slower the cadence. Executives take their time to address an individual or a group. It's a surefire technique for ensuring a captive audience. Wannabes lacking in self-confidence tend to talk at a rapid-fire pace because they fear they will be cut off before they can finish. Usually, they achieve the exact opposite of what they desire.

Silence

Senior executives use strategic silences to appear thoughtful. Don't feel you have to fill in every conversation gap with words.

Grammar

Impeccable grammar is mandatory, particularly for a top executive position. As the corporation's ultimate figurehead, a CEO can seriously embarrass his or her organization by using the wrong verb tense, plural formation, or pronoun case in a public forum—especially with clients or security analysts. Brainpower may have launched many young scientists, engineers, and other "hard skilled" professionals into positions of power and authority, but more often than not they remain frozen two levels below senior management because they continue to use inaccurate grammar. The business caste system is particularly unforgiving to executives who fail to adopt the trappings of the upper middle class, and grammar is a surefire diagnostic.

Profanity

There are no gray areas here. Never swear or curse in the presence of a recruiter. Even though some executives may use foul language when communicating with a small group of high-level internal staff, profanity brands you as an undisciplined maverick with a bad temper.

> *Good communicators answer difficult, probing questions*
> *with comfort and simplicity using language any lay person*
> *can understand.*
> BILL MATTHEWS, PARTNER, HEIDRICK & STRUGGLES

Jargon—apply sparingly

Although every industry, and company for that matter, has its own legitimate jargon, many executives use buzzwords as all-purpose catchalls to demonstrate their linguistic sophistication or to fill in when they can't think of a more precise word. While it's OK to use jargon sparingly to capture a specific thought or to make yourself appear like an industry insider, most recruiters say that the best executives avoid larding their conversations with jargon and use the following words with a light hand:

Added value
Architecture (e.g., systems architecture, decision architecture, compensation architecture, reward architecture)
Change initiative
Competitive advantage
Core
Drive
Facilitate
Impactful
Integration
Interface
Opportunity
Platform
Prioritize
Proactive
Solution capability
Strategic
Value added
Value chain

Recruiter Scorecard: How You Say It

ENHANCERS

Good listening skills

Clarity

Brevity

Vocabulary power

Ability to challenge tactfully

Command of the conversation

DIMINISHERS

Talking too much

Overuse of "I"

Too much jargon

Inability to get to the point

Soft-spokenness

AND NEVER . . .

Come to an interview without prepared questions

Swear

Use incorrect grammar

11

LEADERSHIP PRESENCE PROFILE:

HEIDI G. MILLER

Solid as a rock

One of America's ten most powerful women, Heidi G. Miller is a top finance and risk management expert who today serves as chief financial officer of Citigroup, the world's largest financial institution. As a result of the merger of Citicorp and Travelers Group in 1998, the new Citigroup has combined assets of $73 billion and is second in size only to the Exxon-Mobil merger. Created to provide worldwide consumers and businesses with a one-stop shop for financial services, Citigroup comprises the former Citibank, Travelers Property & Casualty, Travelers Life & Annuity, Salomon Smith Barney, and Primerica Financial Services.

Not only did Miller, forty-six, survive the merger, she is at the control panel for much of the reorganization. As keeper of the company's all-important credit ratings, she draws the hard lines for the still-inchoate organization, which has experienced some bumps, bruises, and defections in its efforts to align. As if her CFO post weren't job enough, she also has a side job: chief risk officer for Travelers' Salomon Smith Barney unit. Although her mentor, Jamie Dimon, president of Travelers, became the merger's highest profile victim in 1998, Miller continues to tough it out successfully with the big boys of finance, like Sandy Weill and John Reed. Says a headhunter who recently tried to recruit her, "She's solid as a rock."

TOUGHING OUT THE CHALLENGES

A member of Citigroup's inner circle, Miller is a high-energy, self-described "doer" known for being calm, focused, and matter-of-fact in a business that can be anything but. No stranger to pressure from flamboyant deal-makers, she has been playing the high-stakes financing game since 1979. Case in point: when Sandy Weill's Travelers Corp. wanted to make a bid for Aetna Property & Casualty in 1995, the deal hinged on lining up $4 billion in financing almost overnight. Weill called in his newly installed chief financial officer, Miller, and told her he was depending on her to save the deal. This required two next-to-impossible tasks: come up with a plan in two days to convince Travelers' banks to underwrite the proposed deal, and even more difficult, ensure that the borrowings wouldn't affect Travelers' credit ratings. If Moody's or Standard and Poor's had seen too much debt they would have downgraded Travelers, increasing the cost of debt and scrapping the deal.

Miller recalls how she toughed out the challenge. "I had to figure out how to finance that sucker. We don't do downgrades, so even a hint of one would have killed the deal." Over a weekend she engineered a complex but brilliant financial solution that coupled the borrowings with two equity offerings, one a private placement, so that the deal wouldn't increase Travelers' debt ratio. And the deal not only preserved Travelers' credit ratings but improved them. Since 1992, Moody's has raised Travelers' credit ratings from Baa1 to Aa3.

CONSUMMATING THE MARRIAGE

Since Citibank and Travelers announced their marriage in spring 1998, the two companies have had a rough time trying to consummate it: the company's investment banking and commercial banking units appear to be culturally incompatible. A member of the "tribe from Travelers," Miller is determinedly imposing a lean, efficient way of operating on Citibank's "big picture" culture that has traditionally ignored the details of day-to-day managing. Some decisions have been easy. Solomon had the powerhouse fixed income business, so it took the lead; Citibank was dominant in international banking, so it assumed command. But other businesses, like derivatives, were harder to call.

As Travelers' knife of efficiency sliced off redundant employees, Citigroup began losing momentum, and in October, 140 Citigroup executives—including Miller—convened at The Greenbrier to get the merger moving again. The result was that 32,000 employees (out of a total of 160,000) were given walking papers. Heidi Miller made the cut, but her mentor, Jamie Dimon, was asked to resign.

Between a 15 percent drop in earnings and the departure of Jamie Dimon, Citigroup's value dropped $11 billion in two weeks, an 11 percent decline. And Miller was left to clean up the mess. "Citigroup's commercial and investment bankers need to begin working together to achieve the full potential of this merger and prevent it from wiping out," says a financial services industry observer.

NO SHRINKING VIOLET

With sterling credentials and more than eighteen years of banking experience, Miller is well suited to the challenge of serving as CFO in a mega merger. But it's not just because of her experience and expertise. Miller's intellect, focus, poise, and communication skills have been key success factors throughout her career. Known as a tough but disarming character, Miller has had to shoulder her way into a macho world with high-paid, ego-driven personalities like Citigroup cochairman Sanford Weill, Dimon—the former president—and Deryck Maughan, vice chairman and former head of Salomon Brothers Smith Barney. As some have observed, "Fail to stand up to them and you're on the carpet. Rub them the wrong way and you have a fight on your hands."

Says Miller, "Being a CFO in a place where everyone acts like a CFO is a tough job," says Miller. "It's not like a manufacturing company. Everyone here has an opinion on liquidity and can read a balance sheet." But she hasn't recoiled from the challenge. Although she is one of a handful of women who are considered truly powerful executives, she is oblivious to her gender—or chooses to ignore it. When asked about how it feels to be a woman in such a high ranking position, she brusquely responds, "Frankly, I don't think about it."

The daughter of a dentist from Queens, New York, Miller got an early taste of working within the boys' club. She was in one of the first classes at Princeton to admit women. "Princeton was such an odd place—there weren't even enough women's bathrooms," she has said. "It made me think a lot about being a woman in a male environment. I rose to the occasion."

THE LATIN AMERICAN CONNECTION

A career in business wasn't Miller's first career choice. When she decided not to follow in her father's footsteps, as he hoped, he agreed to pay for her to attend law school after she graduated from college in 1974. But law didn't much interest Miller. Instead, she elected to put herself through graduate school at Yale and received a Ph.D. in Latin American history in 1979. Her thesis topic? Labor relations in the era of a master of executive presence— Argentinian dictator Juan Peron. It was farewell to academia when no jobs teaching history materialized, but the banking industry was expanding globally and sought recruits who could speak Spanish and knew something about Latin America.

During her thirteen years at Chemical, Miller ascended the corporate hierarchy quickly. The collapse of Latin America's economy threw her onto the bank's fast track. One of her first tasks was representing the bank at debt restructuring negotiations following the Latin American debt crisis that swept through the financial markets. With an understanding of the region developed through her academic studies, Miller saw promise where many saw write-offs. She helped the bank start a Third World debt-trading desk and a corporate finance group that began swapping bad debt for equity stakes in local companies like wineries and insurance firms. "As a historian, I could make a leap between data points and understand the whole picture in a way many people might not," she says. As part of the management team that made a lot of money for Chemical, Miller eventually became managing director and head of the bank's emerging markets structured finance group.

WORK FOR PEOPLE YOU RESPECT
Miller is a tough-minded yet unassuming executive who has worked closely with some of the great minds in financial services. She left Chemical when it merged with Manufacturers Hanover in 1992 and signed on as assistant to Dimon, president of Primerica, the Sanford Weill insurance company that later became Travelers. Her friends, who thought she was taking a job as Dimon's secretary, were dumbfounded. But she saw it as a great opportunity to learn and follow her own modus operandi: work for people you respect. Miller, who describes herself as averse to change, decided to make a move rather than wait out the evolving new structure. By 1995, she was promoted to executive vice president and CFO of Travelers Group.

Since becoming CFO of Citigroup, Miller has been focused on receiving Federal Reserve approval of the merger. Commercial banks and insurance companies are not legally allowed to merge, so Travelers created a bank holding company prior to completing the merger with Citicorp. While Citigroup waits in the hope that Congress will change the law, Miller is responsible for proving that the merged company meets strict reporting requirements. She is also responsible for accounting, treasury, tax, and financial planning and analysis functions at the corporate level. A member of the Citigroup Risk Committee, the Salomon Smith Barney Risk Committee, and the Travelers Property Casualty Risk Committee, Miller now reports to Sandy Weill, CEO of Citigroup.

Miller's name appears regularly on the short lists of many headhunters. Although she hasn't moved from firm to firm like many of her colleagues in financial services, some speculate she may follow her mentor Dimon once he lands on his feet.

LEADERSHIP PRESENCE

Miller's leadership presence is an utter contrast to the flamboyant, charismatic presence of her bosses Sandy Weill and John Reed.

Appearance. In contrast to some highly placed women in the world of high finance, Heidi Miller is unassuming and conservative. "She's not a power dresser—you won't see her in a Chanel suit," says one observer. "She looks more like a librarian."

Poise. Some top professional women on Wall Street have found that a coquettish or flirtatious approach greases the skids in the male-dominated world of high finance. Not Miller, according to observers. "That's her strength," says Scott MacCormack, the *Forbes* reporter who profiled her in fall 1998. "She keeps her head down and gets the job done."

Focus. Once Miller switched from academia to banking, she was committed. "I don't like change very much," she says repeatedly. "My husband says I don't even change lanes on the highway." To make sure no part of the day is wasted, she listens to taped lectures on subjects like philosophy and religion as she drives herself between Manhattan and Greenwich, Connecticut, where she lives with her family.

Passion. In an industry of big, flamboyant personalities, Miller takes a contrarian approach. Her executive presence stems primarily from her levelheadedness and utter lack of ostentation. "She's passionate about being matter of fact and earnest," says one observer.

Charisma. Although the mesmerizing aspects of charisma are not Miller's forte, she's viewed as a people person. "Heidi is very down to earth, serious, and kind," says Scott MacCormack of *Forbes.* "She has served as a mentor to many young people at Travelers, Chemical, and Citigroup. Some might even think of her as maternal."

Intellect. Miller was selected CFO because neither of the merger partners could dispute her brilliance or her ability to get results. "She's smart as hell," says an observer, "and she knows how to get things done in a business that is incredibly complex."

Communication skills. Miller's sense of humor is self-deprecating but dead-on. When queried about her ability to beat near-impossible deadlines and challenges dished to her by mentors Sandy Weill and Jamie Dimon, she shrugs, "I'm a Jewish girl from Queens. I like report cards, and credit ratings are my grades."

Culture fit. Unlike many financial services executives, Miller has spent her entire business career in banking, working for only two companies. The biggest cultural challenge for her, like many Travelers employees, has been addressing Citibank's freewheeling culture and building a mutually beneficial way of doing things that can benefit Travelers, Citibank, and other Citigroup units—without downgrading the debt ratings, of course.

Author's note: at the time this book went to print, Heidi G. Miller had elected to leave Citigroup and join the dot.com industry as chief financial officer of Priceline.com, an Internet retailer.

Career Timeline: Heidi Miller

Education

Princeton University	B.A., History	1974
Yale University	Ph.D., History	1979

Business Experience

1999–present   Priceline.com—Norwalk, CT
Chief Financial Officer

1992–1999   Travelers Group/Citigroup—New York
CFO, Citigroup
1998–present
CFO, Travelers Group
1995–1998
Senior Executive Vice President/Chief Risk Officer
1993–1998
Senior Vice President, Planning & Analysis/Assistant to the President
1992–1994

1979–1992   Chemical Bank—New York
Managing Director & Group Head, Emerging Markets Structured Finance Group
1987–1992
Vice President, Mexican Desk Head
1980–1987
Assistant Vice President, Brazil Desk
1980–1982
Management Trainee
1979–1980

12

HOW YOU
THINK

*Brainpower and the ability to think strategically are a
recruiter's top must-have factors.*

Leadership presence is a melange of many important elements. But second only to past success—the best predictor
of future success—a candidate's brainpower and ability to
think strategically are the most critical factors in his or her
desirability as an executive. Intellect and mental agility
were cited by more of the recruiters than any other factor
in our survey. Assuming a candidate's resume is accurate,
it's easy to assess his or her track record on paper. But
assessing brainpower is best done in person, according to
headhunters and their clients. "Most recruiters aren't
strategic thinkers but they can recognize it," says recruiter
Herman Smith. "Some of my clients and candidates think
on a higher level than I do. I don't necessarily have to

understand what they're saying, but I have to judge their ability to think strategically."

What does thinking strategically mean? And how does a recruiter evaluate an executive's ability to think strategically?

Senior executives aren't paid to make a better widget or sell it to a customer; they're paid to coordinate the multitude of activities that must happen before the widget exists, during its creation, after it's made, when it's sold, and after it's sold. They're paid to look out over the horizon and see not only what competitors are doing, but also how technology, communications, economies, and demographics are shifting and how customers use widgets, widget substitutes, non-widget alternatives and—heaven forbid—no widgets at all. They have to understand the opportunities and threats, identify what *could* be, and outline the path to the goal. And they have to motivate other people to do all the work. "At this level, the risks are highest, the time frames the longest, and the stakes more substantial," says recruiter Jeffrey Christian of Christian & Timbers.

DO YOU HAVE IT?

The ability to think strategically can be inferred from a candidate's resume and from what others have to say about him or her. But most recruiters believe it's important to confirm it in person, to hear the candidate articulate a vision and pathway to the goal. Recruiters and management experts say that tomorrow's leaders will have to chart critical paths through complex global problems. "They won't just have to think out of the box—they'll have to think out of the universe," says Christian. "They need to understand how business models change overnight, and juggle burning torches in twenty-four time zones."

How do recruiters uncover the ability to think strategically? By asking candidates to talk about their accomplishments and discuss hypothetical situations. Candidates demonstrate whether or not they are strategic thinkers by the issues they discuss and the questions they ask. Recruiters listen for cues in seven major areas.

BIG PICTURE THINKING

Recruiters say that strategic thinkers, even if they are worried about short-term earnings or next month's revenues, are able to focus on the big picture when interviewing for a job. They know their job is to make things change—in an orderly, coherent manner. They know they have to envision the future and its consequences before they can move the organization towards the future. And they demonstrate their strategic thinking capabilities by questions such as:

- Why do customers pick one competitor over another?
- What strategies distinguish one competitor from another?
- How will technological breakthroughs affect our industry?
- What other industries offer examples to ours?
- What social and political trends could affect our product and strategy?

In addition, recruiters seek cues from what candidates say. The most successful candidates talk about:

- *Planning vs. doing:* Strategic thinkers talk about scoping out the competition, preparing the work force, upgrading the technology, and selecting the right people for the job before launching into it.
- *Time horizons:* Big picture thinkers believe they have responsibility and accountability over long time frames, often as much as ten years.
- *Strategy vs. tactics or implementation:* Big picture thinkers talk about competitors, external forces, threats and opportunities, human and technological resources, financing considerations, where changes can be made, and how they will affect the bottom line. Tactical thinkers talk about internal procedures, mechanics of the job, reporting relationships, personalities, and budgets.
- *Strategic issues*: Big picture thinkers seek information on the client's strategic issues, as opposed to tactical issues, budget, or compensation.

In addition, big picture thinkers tend to frame their comments in a strategic context by answering the question behind the question. If the recruiter asks, "How would the board of directors rate your performance?" an executive with presence doesn't simply respond, "Very good." Rather, he or she might say, "The board would rate my performance on three criteria: profits, market share, and sales growth. Here's how I accomplished results on each of them."

Finally, big picture thinkers:

- Discuss strategic issues that are affecting their current (or last) organization;
- Inquire about the external and internal forces affecting the client's business;

- Demonstrate some insight into the client's strategic challenges;
- Prepare for the interview by scrutinizing the client's annual report and Web site, studying the position description, and asking questions that line up their experience with the client's strategic issues.

Intellectual curiosity is a key requirement for any CEO. I expect someone at this level to be able to look at issues the way everyone else is looking at them—and to add new dimensions, ways of looking at an issue that aren't obvious to everyone.

PETER D. CRIST, PRESIDENT, CRIST PARTNERS

VISION

Vision is one of the most difficult factors to confirm on paper or even in person. The recruiter may not specifically ask you what your vision of business or management is, but if you don't address it directly, he or she will make a judgment about it from everything else you say.

Although senior executives—particularly CEOs—may have very different approaches for attaining their visions, including fixing, slashing/burning, safeguarding, and building, they *have* a vision, and they're intensely committed to achieving it. Most recruiters and their clients feel it's important for an executive candidate to articulate a vision for their company, department, or function and describe how they have pursued it. It almost doesn't matter what your vision is. But it's important to make it clear you have one. Recruiters report that a vision can be something as simple as:

- Making reputation management the number one priority for your organization;
- Positioning Widget Inc. as the number one producer and marketer of widgets in the Western Hemisphere;
- Transforming a process-oriented culture into a customer-oriented culture.

In addition, you can underscore your visionary capabilities by acknowledging the client's vision, which is typically stated clearly in its latest annual report, and referring to it throughout your conversation, and by seeking more information on how the client's vision is being implemented.

BALANCE

Recruiters love it when candidates address their own strengths, weaknesses, and mistakes. These are among the most important data they must report to their client. Candidates secure enough to point to a few failed projects among the many successful ones build credibility for themselves, show they're human, and most important, demonstrate that setbacks don't impede their progress. "I can't trust an executive who says he's never had a failure," says one recruiter. "You know he's either a finger pointer or totally clueless."

> In person, people tend to shy away from problems. They think that when they have you one on one, they can win you over. But candidates need to do their homework, ask intelligent questions, and accurately describe their role in making accomplishments happen. There aren't too many things that people can tell me that I can't verify.
> CHARLES SPLAINE, PRESIDENT, SPLAINE & ASSOCIATES

Says Dayton Ogden, president of Spencer Stuart, "The candidates who are willing to discuss mistakes, wrong turns, and weaknesses are among the most impressive for three reasons. They demonstrate their flexibility of mind and willingness to shift gears when something changed; they have enough self-confidence to show that they are human; and they provide me firsthand information I would have to extract from a reference at a later point." Ogden recalls interviewing a candidate for a CEO position with a multinational company. "The most impressive thing he did was tell me that he wasted the first three months of his current job because he hadn't conducted due diligence thoroughly enough before pursuing a particular strategy." According to Ogden, the candidate was candid about his strengths and weaknesses as well. "He had enough balance to tell me he would be good at 75 percent of the position because of his past experience, but needed support to accomplish the remaining 25 percent effectively."

> *If you don't understand where some of your significant mistakes were made, there's a problem. If you are not clear on them, you are significantly in denial. We want to hear what people have learned along the way.*
> STEVE MADER, MANAGING DIRECTOR,
> CHRISTIAN & TIMBERS

Other recruiters agree that the ability to describe weaknesses is hugely revealing about a candidate's management style and continuing intellectual growth. "The best people don't just catalog their accomplishments—they also tell you what they've learned from their experiences, good and bad," says Ann Peckenpaugh of Schweichler Associates.

"An ability to talk about their weaknesses realistically demonstrates their intellectual honesty."

Balancers:
- Are prepared to discuss weaknesses or mistakes;
- Describe how they remedied a mistake or problem and what they changed so it wouldn't happen again;
- Discuss how their perspective on an issue changed over time and the impact this had;
- Detail how they addressed mistakes and what they learned from them;
- Pinpoint one or two problem spots at the client company that parallel situations they have addressed and recommend approaches.

What is leadership presence? It's almost impossible to define. Some recruiters depend on "The Look"—presenting candidates who are well-groomed, well-dressed, and tall with brand-name educational credentials and good communication skills. But it's critical to get beyond playing the part. To me, leadership presence is a level of maturity that someone attains after coping with a variety of life experiences. And I have never seen a CEO without a sense of humor.
BILL GOULD, MANAGING DIRECTOR,
GOULD, MCCOY & CHADICK

A sense of humor is another hallmark of a balanced mind. Recruiters say that executives don't demonstrate humor by cracking jokes or impersonating the client's chairman. Rather, they are masters of self-deprecating banter and keen observers of irony or absurdity. Executives with the best people skills use humor to put people at ease.

"They see the funny side of life as well as the analytical side," says Dayton Ogden.

INSTINCT

Senior executives, especially those in general management or CEO positions, don't have time to apply a rational process to all decisions. Although management books recommend making decisions by looking at all the options, identifying the evaluation criteria, weighing the options quantitatively, and selecting the option with the highest score, hardly any practicing executive uses that approach. Another challenging factor for recruiters to assess, gut instinct is the ability to make judgments and decisions without conducting a time-consuming analysis of options. Sometimes called intuition, gut instinct is essentially the scar tissue of experience: the consolidated knowledge about human, market, and political reactions and behavior accumulated over years of trying things and making mistakes. But because a scientific explanation of intuition doesn't exist, many organizations don't trust it.

Recruiters look for evidence that candidates are able to build up experience quickly. Some of the cues they look for include rotations through a variety of jobs and service on high-level project teams, which hone decision-making skills. Exposure to top management, either in a staff role or a top line management position, sharpens a manager's ability to process complex data and deal with multiple constituencies. And the ability to soak up secondhand experience from others quickly builds gut instinct. Recruiters also look for anticipation. Managers with finely tuned instincts are already focusing on challenges they expect to address five years from now.

POLITICAL SAVVY

Strategic thinking requires emotional intelligence as well as intellectual intelligence, according to recruiters. Politically savvy executives accurately read key power relationships and crucial social networks. They understand that every organization, and every recruiter, has implicit ground rules for what is acceptable and what isn't. They also know how the recruiting game is played, and they play along.

According to Daniel Goleman, author of *Working with Emotional Intelligence*, every company has its own invisible nervous system of connections and influence, and the ability to read the political realities is vital to the behind-the-scenes networking and coalition building that allows an executive to wield influence.

Resourcefulness is another aspect of political savvy. Sometimes a company's formal and unwritten rules can present mighty roadblocks to achieving results. While circumventing or ignoring official policy and tradition can diminish credibility and moral leadership, a knack for working around the rules or redefining them to accommodate their agenda can win executives plaudits.

It's critical for aspiring executives to tune into the climate and culture of the company—and into the forces that shape the views and actions of clients, customers, and competitors. It's also essential that they accurately read organizational and external realities.

PLAYING THE SEARCH GAME—NOT

Don't make the mistake of treating a recruiter, particularly one from a retained firm, like an employment counselor. Recruiters consider themselves part of the upper level of the business caste system and hate it when candidates mispronounce or forget their name, discount their role, or assume that they are simply a pipeline to the real decision-maker.

And avoid the temptation to exaggerate or misrepresent. The majority of candidates for executive and professional positions are straightforward with executive recruiters when describing their scope of authority and accomplishments. However, the challenge of beating out a rival often prompts candidates to embellish their achievements to win an offer they may have no intention of accepting. Executive recruiters are skilled in detecting canned responses, hyperbole, or shopworn misrepresentations. Some of the classics, along with how a recruiter is likely to translate them, include:

"As assistant vice president at XYZ Corp., my position is equivalent to a senior vice president on your client's organization chart."

Translation: "I'm one of 400 assistant vice presidents and it looks like I won't be promoted to associate vice president."

"My major weakness is working too much. I just drive myself and my people too hard."

Translation: "If I tell you all my real weaknesses, you'll run away screaming and I'll never get a job."

Alternate translation: "I've just finished reading all the books that I could find on how to ace an interview, and this is what they told me to say."

"My goal is to become CEO."

Translation: "I forgot to think about what my goal is before coming to this meeting."

"Salary range and benefits don't really matter to me. I'm looking for a career opportunity. The job comes first for me."
Translation: "I'm interviewing everywhere I can, and when I'm done with the process, I'll choose the offer with the highest salary."

"I left the company and am currently consulting."
Translation: "There has been a layoff and I got caught in the crossfire. Right now I am unemployed and seeking a new job."

Because this is the usual interpretation, "real" consultants need to be very clear about this distinction. If you are in the job market but have had some serious consulting projects, include an addendum to your resume that describes them. A general overview of your consulting practice, or even a brochure or capabilities sheet, would be a great addition to your resume when considering a full-time position once again.

"I know that the company is not doing well and that there are bound to be layoffs. But, I want to stick around until after they pass out the severance packages."
Translation: "I'm really scared of making a change. I've been here so long that I'd rather wait to be pushed out of the nest than to even think about leaving on my own."

"I'm a big believer that management talent transfers across industries."
Translation: "It hasn't seemed to work to well in my current industry."

"I increased revenues 20 percent last year."
Translation: "I'm not sure what the revenue figure actually was, but the recruiter will really be impressed by this percentage."

A solid candidate for a general management position should be able to construct a matrix showing his company's revenues, expenses, pretax profit, and number of employees over the last five years—from memory. Says recruiter Steve Seiden, "How hands-on is this executive if he can't? He may be just a marketing guy who says he controls the bottom line but doesn't."

DON'T SPILL YOUR GUTS

While it's never wise to lie about your accomplishments or job history, don't be too eager to provide information that might sabotage your candidacy. A month after the head of marketing for a large international consulting firm had been asked to leave because of philosophical differences with the firm's CEO, he was still scrambling to find a new job. With few alternative opportunities available at his compensation range, he was on the verge of taking a middle management job at an ad agency when a recruiter called. Was he interested in joining a major commercial bank as vice president of marketing, with a starting compensation 20 percent higher than his current level?

With no other prospects in sight and mortgage payments looming, the candidate braced himself for one of his toughest acting roles: playing nonchalant. His challenge was to fuel the recruiter's continuing interest while making it appear that he was too important to leave his current situation. Although his resume had been on the street for several weeks, he told the recruiter he didn't have a current version prepared and asked to see the position description for the bank job. The recruiter faxed it to him, the candidate shaped his resume to fit the PD, and in less than two weeks he had an offer from the bank—as well as a signing bonus.

Recruiter Scorecard: How You Think

ENHANCERS

> Good examples and evidence
> Sense of humor
> Curiosity
> Insightful questions
> Ability to acknowledge mistakes
> Learning agility
> Flexibility
> Clarity and depth of thinking
> Imagination

DIMINISHERS

> Inflexibility
> Inability to address strategic questions
> Inability to quantify results
> Unclear thinking
> Inability to substantiate claims
> Focus on past, not future

AND NEVER . . .

> Use canned responses
> Come unprepared

13

THE PASSION
TO LEAD

There are no reluctant leaders. The passion to get up and lead is the single most important factor in the success of a new CEO, or any top executive.

"You gotta want it, and want it bad," says Gerry Roche. "There are plenty of great guys who just don't want it. And if you don't want it, then you don't go after it because it takes passion, drive, and single-minded dedication to get it."

DESIRE TRUMPS ALL

"Even if you're a brilliant navigator and you know how to sail, you have to want to take charge of that boat," says Roche. "If you don't, some extroverted, loudmouth, egotistical, dominating guy will get up and say, 'we're going to go this way.' People will follow him instead of you—no matter how much you know."

Passion and commitment can even compensate for resume weaknesses. Recruiter Bonnie Crabtree of

Korn/Ferry International tells about a candidate who was referred to her for a senior management position. "On paper he wasn't great, and I was mentally prepared to spend as little time as possible with him. Instead, I spent an hour and a half." The reason? His dynamism and enthusiasm. "He walked into the interview room with energy, offered his hand first and said, "Hey Bonnie, how are you, it's great to see you." According to Crabtree, he knew about interviewing and asked strategic questions about how his skills would fit in, what the company's expectations were in the first three months, the first six months, and how it would judge whether or not he was having an impact." Most important, he was sincerely interested.

In contrast, some executives who appear enormously promising on paper undermine their own case because of their phlegmatic temperament. One recruiter recalls conducting a search for the president of a major multinational company's consumer products division. "My candidate was right on spec," says the recruiter. "His resume showed a consistent pattern of increasing responsibility and authority since he graduated from Harvard Business School in the mid-1970s. He had been promoted every three years, was recruited regularly by high-quality organizations, and was currently in a general management position with a global consumer package goods company.

"He seemed like the ideal candidate," says the headhunter. "But when I met him, I was astonished by his nonchalance about his current company's performance and challenges it faced." When the recruiter asked him to describe the single most compelling issue his company now addressed, the candidate said he couldn't think of anything particularly compelling. When he said, "We have everything under control and it's operating like clock-work," the recruiter knew he was either one of the least interesting candidates he had ever interviewed or he was lying. The recruiter axed the candidate and ended up pre-senting three executives with lesser credentials but more enthusiasm.

"If someone comes to a personal interview and doesn't appear to be interested, it's a danger signal," says recruiter Bernadette Pawlik, principal with Pawlik/Dorman Associates in Chicago. "By the time candidates have advanced past the resume and telephone screening, they're usually into the process. They see the recruiter interview as the 'final round' and want to win it."

PASSIONATE CEOS

Passion can't be determined from a resume or a phone conversation, says recruiter Skott Burkland. It can only be determined in a face-to-face meeting. "True leaders, whether in business, government, or other professions, live, dream, and think about their work," says Burkland. "Being a CEO means more to them than just doing the job. It means trying to figure out how they can make a greater contribution and attract equally passionate people to work on the team."

It also means putting in grueling hours. Though most executives were born and raised in an upper-middle-class environment, they often have a "blue collar work ethic that enables them to work around the clock," according to recruiter Dennis Carey of Spencer Stuart. "Executives know that they are on a mission and have an overwhelm-ing need to win. They're like generals in the midst of a full-scale war: they know the stakes are high and they feel it's important to demonstrate to the troops that they are tireless worriers about winning the battle," says Carey. "Sometimes they really do act like generals who never sleep or relax: they summon the troops to the office on the weekend, call them late on Sunday night."

> *What distinguishes successful CEOs is their commitment to the business. The business is their hobby. Everything they do is for the business or to build their knowledge around the business.*
> KATHLEEN JOHNSON, PARTNER, BARTON ASSOCIATES

Passion may not be necessary for a chief financial officer. But it's essential that top executives and general managers demonstrate passion, commitment, and ferocity—the traits of lovers. Says Herb Kelleher, CEO of Southwest Airlines, who is consistently elected one of the best leaders in corporate America, "I love it, I love it—I sure as heck do." According to Warren Buffett, CEO of Berkshire-Hathaway, "Find the leader who loves his business—who's not measuring himself by whether he got into Augusta or goes to Davos." Says Buffett, "I could play golf like Tiger Woods, but if Berkshire were not doing well, I'd not be happy."

FINDING PASSIONATE EXECUTIVES
It's not easy. Amanda Fox, partner with Spencer Stuart's Chicago office, recalls a search to find the CEO for a joint venture between a large management consulting firm and a major commercial bank. "'For this kind of position, a candidate needed enough energy to convince both joint venture partners as well as the employees that he or she

was in charge," says Fox. One candidate was a senior investment banking executive who had been a partner with a Big Six accounting firm and had also served as CEO of a growing health care company. He also had international experience—another requirement of the job. "I went to meet him thinking 'the guy who comes through that door is going to be a real dynamo,'" says Fox. "But in walked Caspar Milquetoast." With a retiring manner, a monotone voice, and an inability to sound or appear excited about any of his past accomplishments, the unimpassioned candidate seemed like a different person from the one on the resume and the phone. As Fox probed his background, it became clear to her that most of his promotions and new positions came on the coattails of his boss or others whom he had served in a "bagman" type role. "A leader of men he was not," says Fox. "He didn't build and shape his jobs and companies—he inherited and managed them."

> *Passion shouldn't be confused with arrogance. Arrogance shows up as weak eye contact, nonstop talking, and saying "I" instead of "we." An arrogant candidate's primary concern is whether the job is big enough for him or her.*
> ANDREA REDMOND, MANAGING DIRECTOR,
> RUSSELL REYNOLDS ASSOCIATES

Passion can also be confused with extroversion. According to Dennis Carey, "A candidate who talks a lot—in a loud tone of voice—is not necessarily passionate. It's certainly possible to demonstrate passion in a quiet way, and executives who follow this model can be even more inspiring than the blow-and-go variety." Carey points to

Stuart Kessler, a CPA who is the lay president of the American Institute of CPAs. "He's a very scholarly man who could be considered almost shy," says Carey. "But he is extraordinarily passionate about the impact that accounting can have on American industry. And he communicates his passion extremely well."

ENERGY

How do recruiters evaluate energy? Many management experts agree that a leader is a key source of his or her organization's emotional tone and excitement. As Birgitta Wistrand, the CEO of a major Swedish company, puts it, "Leadership is giving energy." According to recruiter Fox, energy level is one of the most important predictors of which candidate will fly. "Corporations who recruit from the outside have an enormous number of issues on their plates and they're typically looking for someone with new vitality to recharge the company," she says. "For many companies, a candidate's physical energy is the outward sign of the inner fervor needed to diagnose and treat a complex set of challenges."

Most executives could learn a lesson in energy—and courage—from Carol Bartz, who became CEO of Autodesk, a Silicon Valley software company, in 1993. On her second day at the company, Bartz, a former Sun Microsystems executive, was diagnosed with breast cancer. Figuring that as a new CEO it wasn't the time for her to disappear, she refused to let her illness distract her from her job. She had a stopgap lumpectomy, then worked a month before getting the radical mastectomy she needed.

*In the first thirty to sixty seconds of an interview, I look for
"voltage"—the combined effect of energy level, passion for
one's business, and competitive edge.*
DAVID R. PEASBACK, PRESIDENT AND CEO,
CANNY BOWEN, INC.

Senior executives who are continually on stage and
interacting with other people know that a strong energy level
is essential to set a positive example for the troops and absorb
the inevitable low blows that business throws their way.
Despite self-doubt and concern, the best executives constantly give the impression that they not only know what to
do, but also know how to do it. Most important, they convince their teams that their plans are doable. At the same
time, they have to deal with a continual flow of decisions,
large and small, in a very public forum.

CEO observers are invariably awed by the energy their
subjects demonstrate in all facets of their lives. Few people
have seen General Electric CEO Jack Welch bored or tired.
Ditto for other high profile CEOs like Michael Armstrong
of AT&T, Lou Gerstner of IBM, as well as many other less-
visible top executives.

*Is the candidate energetic, tireless? What are his or her
work habits?*
DURANT A. HUNTER, PRESIDENT AND CEO,
PENDLETON JAMES ASSOCIATES

While energy is a primary component of passion and
executive presence, recruiters want to see that it is well harnessed and under control. Sometimes an executive's

energy level can overwhelm him as well as the headhunter. One recruiter tells about interviewing candidates for a CEO position at a Midwest manufacturing company. "This company was a successful, family owned business. The old man wanted to retire and turn the reins over to a professional manager who could bring energy and fresh blood to fire up a very staid operation. One of our candidates was the number two executive at a Chicago competitor who had been passed over for the top spot at the company." According to the headhunter, the candidate's resume was exceptional, and several references had said he could really stir things up.

"A tornado was more like it," says the recruiter. "He burst into the meeting room like Attila the Hun, slammed the door shut, and gazed around the room until we locked eyes. After a deep breath, he paused, thrust his hand at me, and told me he was Joe Blow and he was here to help me. I asked him to tell me why he was interested in the job, and he launched into a thirty-minute soliloquy, which appeared to be directed at me, the door, the extra chair, his own left hand, and the telephone. The guy just couldn't sit still—he was up and down at least four times during his speech. It was that day that I realized how small a ten by ten room really was."

OPTIMISM AND ENTHUSIASM

One important aspect of passion in a business context is optimism. While Bible thumping doomsayers threatening the fiery furnace may have success motivating sinners to repent, corporate America is no place to scare or depress a company into transformation, particularly in an era of low unemployment and rampant job changing. "The old adage about catching more flies with honey than with vinegar is the essence of management success in today's organizations," says one recruiter. "Honey includes compensation and benefits, but it also includes telling the team they can do more and better instead of reminding them how inadequate they are."

A leader is someone who can translate pressure into positive energy.
KENNETH M. RICH, PARTNER, RAY & BERNDTSON

Recruiter Steven Darter, president of People Management Northeast, once interviewed a candidate who spent an hour itemizing the client's blunders and misjudgments. "He told me he could get it all turned around, but couldn't give me any specific tactics," says Darter. "We crossed him off the list the minute he left the room." It's OK to express concerns about some aspect of the potential employer's strategy, product line, or operations—particularly if you can suggest another approach that works better. But don't let the interview devolve into a critique session. Employers want managers who are excited by opportunities, not dismissive of past mistakes. If you have qualms about the company's problems, voice them in a positive, or at least concerned, manner.

The higher you go in an organization, the more important your selling and persuading skills are—internally as well as externally. After all, the CEO is his or her company's top sales person—to customers, stockholders, employees, legislators, the media, and other important constituencies. And research has shown that optimism is essential to strong sales performance. Metropolitan Life, for example, tested salespeople for optimism to determine its effect on sales performance. Salespeople who scored high for optimism sold 37 percent more insurance than the pessimists did. Optimist applicants who failed to meet Metropolitan Life Insurance Company's other standard test criteria were hired anyway. This group outsold its pessimistic counterparts by 21 percent its first year and by 57 percent the next. And optimism can be taught. There are books devoted to the subject.

FOCUS

Recruiters look for candidates with strong concentration skills because the ability to focus is another key element of emotional intelligence. Leaders are rarely distractible: they have the ability to consider a single issue with 100 percent attention while hundreds of other issues process in the background. They lean forward slightly when they sit—a mark of attentiveness—and they listen carefully. They also have a knack for boiling down an issue to its fundamental points quickly and elegantly. They get to the heart of the matter quickly.

Lack of focus knocked a top candidate for a CFO position at a major consumer products company off one search firm's list. Although the candidate had the right experience and presence, he interrupted the forty-five-minute interview with the recruiter three times to answer his mobile phone. Two of the calls concerned home plumbing repairs.

Bob Clarke, who recruits for managed care companies and medical professionals, recalls interviewing a physician for a position as a medical director in a large practice. "He had his beeper on and took calls during the interview," said Clarke. "Although he had great credentials, I crossed him off my list. Not only was it rude to me, it was unprofessional: a doctor shouldn't make other commitments when he is on call."

CONTROLLED APPETITE FOR RISK

Like anything in which passion is involved, running a business involves some risk. Typically, a company doesn't call an executive recruiter unless it wants to explore a different strategy or an "out of the box" solution—a risky but potentially rewarding approach that an insider cannot typically provide. Many newly formed companies, by definition risky propositions, recruit executives from the outside to acquire the experience and knowledge necessary for building an organization.

Judging a candidate's appetite for risk is one of the most challenging duties of an executive recruiter. Many headhunters believe that the longer executives work in large corporations, the less appetite for risk they are likely to have. Experience in a big organization always provides a strong grounding in basic management skills, but it makes managers increasingly risk averse. Recruiter Fred Siegel recalls conducting a search for the CEO of a $5 million startup company. "The candidate had a perfect background, solid education, polished appearance, excellent communication skills, and the poise and charisma necessary for a top leadership position," says Siegel. "But he was needy. Coming from a large company, he was used to all types of support and afraid of risk."

"Although there are some exceptions, most megacompanies allow for a bigger margin of error and have more places to hide mistakes and dead bodies," says another recruiter. "In a smaller company, executives are responsible for a wider band of activities and they have to make more decisions faster, with less information." According to the recruiter, it's almost impossible to find an executive from a large corporation with enough risk tolerance to run a new venture. "If our client needs a general manager for a new joint venture, we look for executives who have managed new business units within large companies, or ones who have cycled back and forth between large and small companies."

When recruiting executives for senior management positions, headhunters look for people who are fascinated by risk and can talk about it freely. Says Netscape CEO Jim Barksdale, "Fear of failure is the thrill that gets your heart rate up." In fact, some recruiters actively seek executive candidates motivated by the paradoxical combination of desire for risk and fear of failure. According to Steven Mader, managing director of Christian & Timbers's Boston practice, the ideal candidate for a CEO of a venture capital backed startup is someone who had a career in a large company and then launched a small company and flopped badly. "Now they're hungry—and knowledgeable," says Mader. "Private investors love to get their hands on someone who is coming off a first error because their motivation level couldn't be higher."

Recruiter Scorecard: Passion

ENHANCERS
>	Enthusiasm for challenges
>	Eye contact
>	Ability to concentrate
>	Magnetism
>	Optimism
>	Intensity
>	Taking charge of interview
>	Ability to translate pressure into positive energy

DIMINISHERS
>	Rambling
>	Low energy level
>	Hurriedness
>	Poor eye contact
>	Distraction

AND NEVER . . .
>	Act like you don't care
>	Fidget
>	Become rattled

14

CHARISMA

A remarkable ability to get others to endorse your ideas and promote them passionately.

The recruiter heaved a sigh of relief as his candidate walked out of the jetway. Every candidate he had interviewed for the CEO position had an "on-spec" resume. But this candidate looked like a CEO.

The search, for the top executive at an electronic component manufacturer based in the upper Midwest, had been a grueling one. Few top candidates were interested in moving from the West or East Coasts. Most of the other candidates didn't have the communication skills, strategic viewpoint, or industry experience to do the job. Many of them simply didn't look the part, either, and the company's board was insistent that the new CEO have the stage presence and communication skills to appeal to a wide range of audiences.

It looked like the answer to the recruiter's prayers was here. Tall—over six feet—slim, healthy and active, a full head of hair with a little gray at the temples, the candidate recognized the recruiter and strode briskly over, arm extended for a bone-crunching handshake. "Fred—great to meet you," he smiled. "I'm looking forward to talking with you."

But ten minutes later, in the Admiral's Club conference room, the recruiter's relief turned to frustration. After complaining bitterly about the first-class service on the flight, the candidate started in on his current employer, their philosophical differences, his clearly superior perspective on what his company needed, and his lack of confidence in his staff, most of whom had been assigned to him when he was recruited to the company two years ago. He was looking forward to getting it all behind him and taking on the new career opportunity that the recruiter was here to offer him.

In another search, recruiter Steven Darter of People Management Northeast recalls flying to meet a candidate for a position as regional sales director for a large insurance company. "On paper, the guy was excellent, and he sounded solid over the phone," says Darter. "But when he walked through the door in a plaid suit, lopsided eyeglasses, and bushy hair pointing every which way, my immediate thought was Larry from the Three Stooges." Despite his unorthodox appearance, the candidate was one of the best Darter had ever interviewed. "He was warm and engaging, knowledgeable, and sincerely interested in the opportunity. And then I discovered three other companies were trying to recruit him as well."

Like any leadership quality, charisma has a sinister side—think Charles Manson, televangelists, or sociopaths—but most recruiters say charisma is a desirable characteristic for executives, provided it's used appropriately and applied consistently. Why? Because it suggests a remarkable ability to get others to endorse your ideas and promote them passionately. According to Jeffrey Sonnenfeld, who chairs Emory University's Center for Leadership and Career Studies, when an executive is perceived to have charisma, his or her business performs better. Direct reports feel inspired. Excitement cascades though the organization.

SHOWHORSE VS. WORKHORSE

While celebrity executives like Herb Kelleher of Southwest Airlines, Jim Barksdale of Netscape, and the late Sam Walton of Wal-Mart are larger-than-life personalities who exuded charisma, today's rising managers may be cut from a different cloth. America Online's Steve Case, who is in the process of taking over Barksdale's company, is known for communicating with customers via electronic mail and is more comfortable facing a computer monitor than a crowd. And many observers say that the latest crop of CEOs have made a decision to put the high-profile part of their job—promoting big visions, briefing Wall Street, restructuring corporations, appearing in company advertising—on the back burner and focus on the workhorse aspects. Paul Walsh, CEO of Pillsbury, says, "Being in the limelight makes people want to take a shot at you." And in an era of employee empowerment, CEOs need to cast off their big shot image in order to communicate with the troops. Even business schools emphasize hard skills, compliance, and consensus management. Emory's Sonnenfeld says you don't hear much about charisma in business schools. "Most leadership courses focus on 'follower-ship,' instead of leadership. The result is a guerrilla war against charisma."

Headhunters agree that charisma is less about the "showhorse" aspects of leadership than the "workhorse" aspects: creating momentum, bringing dynamism to the job, and generating energy in other people. It also means:

- The ability to bring people together to get things done and pay attention to everyone who's involved in the project;
- Understanding the people who are following you, why they are following you, what's in it for them, and how you can help them;
- Demonstrating how serious you are about building momentum in the organization, appearing interested, caring, and concerned. Charlotte Beers, former chairman of Ogilvy & Mather, defines charisma as "wit, humor and the ability to express joy."

Recruiters agree that assessing charisma in a one-on-one interview is a challenge, but they nonetheless look for critical cues. Remembering names, cordiality, and empathy are all important. So is extroversion: charismatic executives usually like to have people around them and mention others in conversation. They say "we" more than "I." They avoid conceptual language and talk about people using several key phrases: "I understand," "I feel," "I sense . . ."

THE POWER OF OPTIMISM

Optimism—seeing the glass half full—is also strongly correlated with charisma. When one recruiter's top candidate spent more than half the personal interview complaining about her current boss and her company's misguided strategy, "It was clear she was charismatically impaired," says one recruiter. As a result, she fell to the bottom of the candidate list and wasn't even presented to the client.

As optimists, charismatic executives are not afraid to address unpleasant news. Says recruiter Brian Sullivan, one of Wall Street's top headhunters, "Anyone can point out the bad stuff and whine about it. Leaders with charisma talk about the bad things that have happened in their business and what they're going to do about it. Chase's stock lost 40 percent of its value in fall 1998. Everyone's net worth was annihilated. But charismatic executives will say, 'We've all been hurt, but we're going to tackle the problems in an upbeat fashion. We need to be motivated, pitching business—and our clients need us too.' That's leadership."

SIMPLE MESSAGES

Charismatic executives have a remarkable ability to distill complicated ideas into digestible messages by simplifying and exaggerating. Jack Welch, CEO of General Electric, sent a clear message to the company's employees, from factory workers to senior management, when he rolled out his "number one or number two" strategy that called for fixing, shutting down, or selling any business that wasn't first or second in worldwide market share. Ronald Reagan captured Americans at all levels with a stripped-down rallying cry of "strong defense and less government." And Netscape CEO Jim Barksdale's message couldn't be more plain: "Netscape everywhere."

Whether you're on the buy or the sell side, success hinges on an ability to influence people through a clear and coherent explanation of ideas. There are many failed financial products and instruments that could have been successful—had they been properly launched and marketed persuasively.
BRIAN M. SULLIVAN, PRESIDENT,
SULLIVAN & COMPANY

Recruiters assess an executive's ability to deliver simple messages by comparing what you say to how long it takes you to say it. Says recruiter Jeffrey Christian, who works primarily at the CEO level, "The essence of leadership is the ability to paint a message crisply." This means an ability to describe your accomplishments and value through a highly condensed, persuasive, and interesting story—not an unshaped torrent of detail. It means using simple, nontechnical language that workers at all levels can comprehend. For purposes of a recruiter interview, it means reducing philosophies, strategies, and tactics to sound bites that make it easy for the recruiter to package you in a way his or her client can best digest your information.

One candidate, a senior vice president of manufacturing at a major chemical company, was on the list for the CEO position at a smaller company seeking someone with big company experience and management skills. "He had a fabulous background, but he had difficulty describing what he was doing without using complicated scientific terminology," says the recruiter. "He couldn't get to the point, and didn't address the needs of the company's customers—external and internal. And he certainly couldn't talk about his career goals in a nutshell."

PEOPLE SKILLS

In a search for the division president of a Fortune 500 company, the first candidate held an MBA degree from Stanford and had twelve years of increasingly responsible assignments at two companies. Candidate number two had joined a large management consulting firm directly after receiving his MBA from Harvard, cycled back into management as a chief strategist for a large company for three years, and returned to consulting. He had become a partner after eight years. "Both men were highly qualified to do the job, and both had exceptional credentials," says the recruiter. "But when I interviewed them, there was no contest. In what he said and how he said it, the first candidate clearly had superior people skills. He smiled. He made an effort to appear interested. He asked what impact my client's strategy was having on its people. He wanted to discuss how the client viewed improvements in technology that could accelerate its production process. And he used humor to point out the inconsistencies in my client's marketing strategies."

In contrast, candidate number two was arrogant and abrupt. "He pulled out a written list of problems my client had and went over them with me, line by line, to discuss how they expected him to solve the problem. Although he showed up for the interview, it was clear that he felt he was doing me a favor."

If you're as bright as they get, you don't have to work at your intellectual acuity. You need to develop human sensitivity and sharpen your people skills as much as you can.
GERRY ROCHE, CHAIRMAN, HEIDRICK & STRUGGLES

People skills are a key cue for recruiters, and without them, few executives have the ability to influence or persuade others to their viewpoints. As corporate hierarchies have fallen, even intellectual stars must solicit help from others and work in teams. They must learn how to persuade, listen, exercise patience and restraint, offer sympathy, feel empathy, and recover from the emotional assaults common to group give-and-take. Many recruiters have seen executives with superb technical expertise who neglected their people skills, and suffered the consequences. No matter how brilliant they are, they are usually passed over or even fired by a former antagonist who can't stand having them around any more. While people skills are clearly essential to CEOs and other top-level executives, they are increasingly essential for anyone who manages other people and wants to do it well. And it's especially important to demonstrate your people skills when you're talking to a recruiter.

You can't be a charismatic executive without honing your people skills, according to recruiters. Finance, accounting, information technology—almost any kind of intellectual skill—can be taught, for a price. People skills, however, are largely self-taught, and many smart, highly successful people forget to teach themselves. Recruiter Christian, says he looks for the ability to create an emotional link between people and ideas.

Recruiters say that charismatic executives demonstrate their people skills in four basic areas: empathy, developing others, customer orientation, and political savvy.

EMPATHY

Charismatic executives are attentive to emotional cues and listen well. They show sensitivity and understanding of others' perspectives. And they offer help based on an understanding of people's needs and feelings.

> *Executives with presence are courteous to people of all levels.*
> *No matter how high and mighty they are, they listen even if*
> *they have 30 things that are more important to think about.*
> DAYTON OGDEN, PRESIDENT, SPENCER STUART

During a search for the division president position at a large consumer package goods company, one recruiter was excited to find a candidate who appeared to be superbly qualified for the position. "This was a tricky assignment, because it was clear the client company was going to have to downsize or restructure within the next two years in order to stay competitive," says the recruiter. The company wanted to hire an outsider to do the dirty work—and they were hoping to find someone who had managed a restructuring in a humane way.

One candidate had a "'spot-on" background and was well regarded in his field. The candidate made a strong first impression and impressed the recruiter with his poise and conversational skills. "It was clear that he was used to holding a CEO-level job and could handle questions with ease, tact, and crispness," said the recruiter. "But the guy was all head. He talked at length about how the restructuring he had put in place reduced fat and improved productivity, but didn't mention once how it impacted the lives of the four hundred people who were laid off. And when we checked references, it turned out that he was known for being a hard-liner, someone who was tough on employees," says the recruiter. Although the candidate's technical skills were superior, the recruiter could not in good conscience recommend him for the position.

DEVELOPING OTHERS

Charismatic executives put a high priority on acknowledging and rewarding people's strengths and weaknesses. They value giving, and receiving, feedback about needs for further growth and improvement. And they are committed to mentoring or coaching other people and giving them assignments that challenge and foster their skills. Although charismatic executives may not spend extensive time coaching and mentoring, they are skilled at counseling their direct reports and sharing their own feelings.

A mid-size investment house was seeking a managing partner to build a new mergers and acquisitions business and expand the firm's services. The firm didn't want a prima donna who would handle everything himself and leave in a few years. Rather, they were looking for a business builder who could create an operation that would thrive, even if he left. "Whoever was chosen would have to pull in other talent, from inside the firm as well as the outside, and shape their skills and client development capabilities," says the recruiter. "We found plenty of bright, interested candidates who could have done the first part of the job—starting an M&A unit. But we had a helluva time finding someone who was a great team leader willing to spend time hiring, giving feedback, and encouraging others to follow in his footsteps."

CUSTOMER ORIENTATION

Charismatic executives understand customers' needs and match them with their company's services or products. They seek ways to increase customer satisfaction and loyalty. And they're able to grasp the customer's perspective. "Most successful CEOs spend a huge chunk of their time working with customers or thinking about customers," says Orit Gadiesh, chair of management consulting giant Bain & Company. "I constantly try to think, 'If I were the customer, how would I feel about this?'"

Recruiter Scorecard: Charisma

ENHANCERS

> Intensity
> Drive
> Determination
> Simplify and exaggerate
> Focus on the future
> One-page charts

DIMINISHERS

> Focusing on details
> Forty-page reports
> Sixty-minute speeches

AND NEVER . . .

> Try to convince someone through logic

15

CULTURE FIT

Whether you're CEO or one of 100 assistant vice presidents, you won't be successful unless you play by the rules. Even if your mandate is to change the rules, you have to change them playing by the current rules.

Companies often hire someone "new and different" from the outside to enhance their market position or stimulate a floundering operation. But even brilliant managers can fail if they accomplish their goals by destroying the organization's cultural fabric. One recruiter recalls a large banking client who wanted to combine the organization's fourteen marketing units into one corporate group headed by a senior vice president. "Their goal was to bring some consistency to the bank's marketing activities and use their collective buying power to reduce advertising and sales promotion expenses," says the recruiter.

The recruiter and his client determined that no one inside the bank had the broad perspective and "boardroom

presence" needed for working with the president and rop-
ing in all marketing programs conducted by the business
lines. Instead, the president of a prestigious advertising
agency that had done extensive work for several of the
bank's units was hired as senior vice president of marketing. "He bombed in less than six months," says the
recruiter. "Although he had the smarts and was sold on the
vision, his style of accomplishing results didn't work
within the bank's organizational structure, which had dot-
ted lines running all over the place. Without direct authority over anyone, he lacked the political clout needed to
persuade the individual units that working through him
was in their best interest. He couldn't get any of the business lines to buy into a common marketing theme and syn-
chronize their marketing efforts." According to the
recruiter, the bank has since abandoned the idea of central-
izing marketing.

Outsiders can often bring needed expertise, contacts,
or management know-how that would take years to
develop internally. But recruiters know that imported
executives won't accomplish much unless they recognize
the organization's intractable cultural patterns. That's why
they look for executives who are a good culture fit, sharing
values, operational behaviors, and attitudes about change
with those of the prospective employer.

Cultural issues have played a role in the failure or
unraveling of numerous high profile alliances such as
BellSouth's major software development deal with Oracle
Corp., and the colossal merger between TCI and Bell
Atlantic. Likewise, cultural friction can undermine a new
executive's ability to make an impact.

At its most basic, corporate culture is "how we do things around here," and new executives, whether a CEO or one of 100 assistant vice presidents, won't be successful unless they play by the rules. Even if their mandate is to change the rules, they won't be successful unless they do it playing by the current rules.

Many recruiters try to make decisions about a candidate's management style, culture, people skills, performance, and suitability in the abstract. The important issue is what does the client think?
DICK CRONIN, PRESIDENT,
HODGE-CRONIN & ASSOCIATES, INC.

Company size plays a major role in its culture. According to recruiter John Martin of J3, a Dallas-based firm, small companies are focused on selling their product and staying alive, and aggressively resistant to the overhead-heavy culture typical of large companies. "Most small companies and startups don't believe in overhead. They don't want to bring in someone from Hewlett-Packard because people who work there have another mindset." An executive accustomed to multiple management layers and lots of staff would likely be uncomfortable with the hands-on, do-it-yourself approach typical of smaller companies, according to Martin.

Culture fit with the organization's board of directors or the hiring manager is also key. Executives hire people in their own image and are more likely to offer a job to someone with similar experience, education, and lifestyle—not to mention the same fraternity. For the savvy candidate, these realities call for some in-depth research on the company prior to the recruiter interview. A little understanding of an organization's culture and the management style of its key managers can help you present yourself most effectively.

DETERMINING CULTURE FIT

Recruiters say that candidates who follow three basic rules will be more likely to select a culture that best fits their distinctive talents and abilities.

Recognize cultural differences. Matching a candidate with a company on paper is easy compared to meshing their cultural background and management styles. Flagging the cultural issues in the early stages of a search can allow the candidate, recruiter, and company to part ways amicably.

Compare cultures. Although cross-industry recruitment is increasing, an executive's success in one industry does not guarantee success in another. If you are considering making a move outside your current industry, carefully compare your management style, decision-making habits, communication approach, and administrative support needs with those of the company that is recruiting you.

Look for culturally diverse leadership. Executives who have succeeded in different environments—like Leo Mullin of Delta—are typically more willing to accept management talent from outside the industry.

MANAGEMENT STYLE

Management style is probably the most important aspect of culture fit. It's not a fancy name for personality. Few recruiters believe that leadership style is a matter of personality, and few believe you have to be "born with it."

Personality is an element of effective leadership, but it's often not the decisive one. According to Carol Hymowitz, who writes regularly on leadership for *The Wall Street Journal*, leaders don't share a particular personality. Recent research suggests that leadership is driven not so much by what someone is like inside but by what the outside demands. Some executives are evenhanded and jocular, others quick-tempered and abrasive. Yet personalities of all types can inspire those who follow them to take risks and do more than they ever thought possible.

In the most successful companies, the CEO has scrutinized the business situation, determined what the organization requires from its leader, and chosen the leadership approach that best meets those requirements. Sometimes the approach fits the CEO's personality; sometimes it does not. Some very good leaders repress certain personality traits or develop ones they weren't born with, in order to run their organizations effectively.

A search assignment presents a similar challenge. The most successful candidates research the management style of the company that wants to hire them. When they meet with a recruiter, they showcase attributes and accomplishments that suit the company's management style and suppress personality factors that may clash.

While every company has a spectrum of management styles, most successful organizations fall into one of six basic approaches, according to research by Bain & Company, Inc.:

Structure management. Every company has procedural, financial, and cultural controls to which members of the organization must conform. But structurers view these tasks as their primary responsibility. Research shows that this approach occurs most often in highly regulated industries, such as banking, or in industries in which safety is a paramount concern, such as airlines, where there is virtually no margin for error, a reality that turns the design and application of strict controls into management's highest priority. As a human being, Richard Rosenberg of BankAmerica is relaxed, flexible, and collegial. The management style he has put in place at BankAmerica is anything but: highly structured, closely controlled by rules and regulations, highly regulated. Rosenberg has been quoted as saying "I fit in a lot better with the people in marketing, but BankAmerica owes it to its customers to have a strict set of controls."

Strategic companies plot their short- and long-term strategic path by gathering vast amounts of data. For instance, Dell Computer, which assembles personal computers, has specially trained employees who take 50,000 phone calls from customers every day and organize their comments for distribution to managers. CEO Michael Dell says that the point is to sensitize the entire organization to the customer. "We want to make everyone literally hear the voice of the customer, to hear the frustration when we do something that makes it difficult to use our products." Phone calls from customers are also used to spark ideas for new products and services.

Human-assets managers communicate and demonstrate what they want face to face. Their travel schedules rival those of a secretary of state or foreign minister, with as much as 90 percent of their time spent out of the office. "People have asked me time and again, 'Why do you spend all that time traveling?' And the answer to that is really kind of simple," says Al Zeien, CEO of Gillette, the personal care products company with 34,000 employees worldwide. "I travel because that's where the people are. I travel because I want to be sure that people who are making the decisions in, say, Argentina have the same reference base as I do for the company. I want to make sure they are all using the same ground rules I would use. I want to see if they have the same objectives. I travel because you can only find these kinds of things on the home ground."

Human-assets companies tend to focus on hiring and training. Wayne Calloway of Pepsico, like many other human-assets CEOs, also occasionally monitors hiring at lower levels of the organization. Similarly, Herb Kelleher of Southwest Airlines says that he has participated in the selection of ramp agents at small regional airports. Hiring, he explains, is "where it starts. It's the head of the river, and if you pollute that, then you gradually pollute everything downstream." Speaking more generally of his approach to leadership, Kelleher sounds another theme of human-assets CEOs: "We hire great attitudes, and we'll teach them any functionality that they need."

Although most human-assets companies tend to value employees who display predictable "company way" values such as honesty and loyalty to the corporation, they also believe in individual empowerment. They can and do give authority to members of the organization to act quickly and freely, without corporate approval, but only to those who conform to the company's way of doing things.

A small but distinct portion of companies foster *expertise management*, which is based on selecting, cultivating, and spreading a competitive expertise up, down, and across the business units of the organization. Expertise companies work to create a specific capability that will allow the organization to differentiate itself from its competitors and lead to a position of sustainable advantage. Expertise can be a package of ideas and techniques, such as the focus on the brand–consumer relationship that drove the leadership of Charlotte Beers, former CEO of the international advertising agency Ogilvy & Mather. Expertise can also be a concept. At Motorola, CEO Robert Galvin's commitment to unassailable quality defines the work of the corporate office. Expertise managers focus on shaping corporate policies that will strengthen their organizations' competencies. Galvin would walk out of meetings about a business unit's performance after quality figures were discussed, vividly demonstrating what he deemed the company's unique competence and his number one concern.

Change agent companies often combine consensus building with another, somewhat contradictory technique: occasional public and dramatic displays of top management's strong support for new ways of doing business. At Tenneco, CEO Dana Mead sets virtually unattainable financial targets for the business units and then actually incorporates them into the budget. He requires Tenneco's five divisional CEOs to give monthly presentations about their performance relative to those targets in an open forum. "The pressure this builds is terrific, and it works," he notes.

Change agents are distinct in their enthusiasm for the kinds of individuals who are often unwelcome in other types of organizations. They tend to value recalcitrant types, troublemakers, or gadflies. According to Debra Germaine, who recruits extensively in the high-tech sector as a partner with Fenwick Partners/Heidrick & Struggles, "Clients will sometimes ask for a candidate who is a 'wild duck' from Hewlett-Packard. What they want is someone who doesn't genuflect to the corporate hierarchy, someone who challenges the status quo. Although they're a bit risky, wild ducks can often launch some exciting projects and deliver exceptional results."

Executives who accept the role of change agent take on perhaps the most demanding and daunting of the six management approaches, according to researchers, because change is almost always accompanied by controversy, discomfort, and resistance. Recruiter Don Clark tells about a search for a new top executive at a staid financial services organization. His candidate was a well-regarded executive from another industry that had experienced many of the market pressures that now faced the banking industry. "Unlike many outsiders, he wasn't turned off by banking as an industry. He was, however, skeptical about the bank's appetite for change," says Clark. "He wanted to know how its culture worked. Most of his questions focused on how open-minded the organization would be about making some major changes. He wanted to be sure he would have access, information, and decision-making ability, and that the bank was sincerely interested in change."

Traditional companies are a dying breed, but they still exist in some industries and areas of the country. Based on the organizational pyramid, they're staffed by executives who have typically spent their careers in a manufacturing company, often rust belt, or large financial institutions, particularly commercial banking. These executives have progressed up the corporate ladder, gaining more support staff with each move. Although they usually have mobile phones, they often don't use a computer because they "don't know how to type." If they do have a computer, they have a secretary print their e-mails. Communication with employees is typically not a priority for these executives, who focus primarily on their boss and board of directors. While traditional managers might like the up-or-out culture of a typical manufacturing organization, for example, they would probably have a hard time adjusting to the team-oriented, decentralized climate of a software company or a service organization.

ENTERING A NEW CULTURE

Vertical careers—those that begin and end in the same industry—are still the norm for the majority of managers. But as Lou Gerstner, Bruce Harreld, and other top-level industry switchers make their name outside their "mother" business, today's employers are increasingly reaching out beyond their industry for professional talent, recruiting candidates who, in an earlier era, would be considered "job hoppers."

Headhunters say that ideal candidates for general management positions at mid-size or large organizations have jumped around several corporate ladders, in the United States and abroad, demonstrating upward mobility in a variety of areas. The candidates who get snapped up fastest? "Those with three- to four-year stints in different functional areas and companies," says recruiter Chip McCreary of Austin-McGregor International. Those who have the hardest time moving up? "The ones who have served in one function or company for a long time," he adds.

Sometimes a transfer seems incongruous. When Peter Larson, Johnson & Johnson's top marketing executive, switched from headache remedies to bowling balls after sporting goods manufacturer Brunswick Corporation selected him as CEO, eyebrows throughout corporate America shot up. But over the last several years, Larson has helped Brunswick increase its market capitalization by almost $2 billion and gross profits by 25 percent.

Several trends have created an ideal climate for advancing through the zigzag method:

Economic growth. The current job market is the hottest in at least a generation: for professionals and managers, the unemployment rate is less than 2 percent nationwide. At the same time, companies that downsized middle management during the re-engineering era face a shortage of promotable executives. While most organizations prefer leaders who combine functional expertise and industry experience, the scarcity of available talent is forcing them to hire candidates with unorthodox backgrounds.

Deregulation is a lightning rod for functional transfers. Managers from the transportation industry, one of the first to deregulate, have moved successfully into telecommunications and other businesses that are entering the private sector. After helping Conrail struggle through deregulation in the late 1970s, its vice president for strategic planning, Leo Mullin, became chairman and CEO of American National Bank from 1991 to 1993 and led First Chicago to a pre-eminent position in commercial banking from 1993 to 1995 as president and COO. After two years as vice chairman of Chicago utility Unicom Corporation, Mullin returned to transportation in 1997 as president and CEO of Delta Airlines.

The convergence of service and manufacturing companies makes career switching a logical consequence. As manufacturers increasingly focus on higher margin business,

leaders with marketing savvy can help position and promote new product/service mixes. The best managers
often come from consumer products companies, where
marketing is a science. Lou Gerstner, who ran consumer
products giant RJR, brought marketing expertise and a
sorely needed new perspective to floundering computer
giant IBM, which is now focusing on the service side of
its business.

> *As a general rule, gathering cross-functional expertise should
> be done as early as possible in the executive's career, as the
> opportunities are more numerous near the base of the corpo-
> rate hierarchy.*
> HOBSON BROWN JR., PRESIDENT AND CEO,
> RUSSELL REYNOLDS ASSOCIATES

Re-engineering backlash. The message companies
preached over the past decade—down with lifetime
employment, up with self-taught, portable skills—has
encouraged career switching and industry transfers. A
1998 study by Aon Consulting, a specialist in human
resource issues, shows that more than half of American
workers will leave their jobs for a pay raise of 20 percent
or less. Says Dr. David Stum, Aon's president, "Today's
workers have become more mobile and assertive. They're
saying, 'I have an offer somewhere else. It's not personal.
It's business.' " And experts advise ambitious managers to
use their current employers as a career steppingstone.
John Humphrey, CEO of management development
consultants Forum Corp., Boston, tells executives to
work for companies where they can build "toolbox skills"
to carry to their next job.

AVOIDING CULTURE SHOCK

Executive recruiters wouldn't be in business if they didn't believe in advancing through the zigzag method. But it inevitably involves some culture shock, particularly at the top management level. Headhunters advise candidates to remember several realities:

Marketing and finance positions transfer best. Any position that has a direct impact on the bottom line transfers more easily than production, manufacturing, or staff positions. Bruce Harreld, president of Boston Chicken, joined IBM as chief strategist in 1995. A marketing genius who positioned the restaurant chain as a nationwide metaphor for high quality takeout food, Harreld has revitalized IBM's market position. Similarly, a background in finance is easily transferable among capital intensive organizations where heavy investment in equipment, capital markets experience, and financial controls can significantly affect profitability. Most airline, manufacturing, and chemical companies have large finance departments and are headed by former chief financial officers.

Technology expertise is hot—if you're not just a techie. Technology managers who can demonstrate real business savvy and an understanding of how systems can help their companies generate revenues can move into general management. Mike Armstrong, who was chairman and CEO at Hughes Electronics, made a successful transition from an engineering-dominated firm to the consumer-oriented telecommunications industry as chairman and CEO at AT&T.

It is possible to transfer classic staff functions. Communications, human resources, and other staff functions can transition across industry lines—but mainly at very senior levels where establishing a functional structure or overhauling the process are more crucial than specific content knowledge. Sandra Allen, formerly director of communications for Commonwealth Edison in Chicago, was recently hired to head corporate communications for the $60 billion Associates Corporation, a financial services company based in Dallas.

Consulting can provide a career transition phase. "If you are a staff executive with no prospects of ascending the hierarchy, consider a stint as a revenue generator in a consulting firm," says Jodi Holden, national staffing manager for KPMG Peat Marwick's consulting division. "More than 90 percent of people we hired last year were midcareer switchers looking for a fast launch to the general management level." Lou Gerstner (IBM), Harvey Golub (American Express), and Michael Jordan (CBS), all alumni of the major management consulting firms, fill the executive suites of corporate America because they're used to working there. Trained ruthlessly to see the big picture, consultants gain visibility working with top management and build a track record of managing people, projects, and budgets.

Establish functional credibility in a conventional corporate setting. There's no substitute for two to four years of credential building in a Fortune 500 or "most admired" company, say recruiters and career switchers. A three- or four-year stint at a major organization can provide access to a broad spectrum of career opportunities.

Dave Holmes, CEO of Reynolds & Reynolds, a producer of business forms and computer systems for auto dealerships in Dayton, Ohio, was hired because of the marketing expertise he gained at General Electric and General Foods, where he launched Shake 'n Bake. One recruiter recalls a partner in a regional management consulting firm who was offered a position as top marketing executive for a Dallas-based money center bank because of the four-year stint she spent at Citibank twelve years earlier.

Switch to companies in which your function is a core skill. In capital intensive businesses, finance executives often rise to the top. In consumer products companies, marketing is key. And in a growing number of American companies, technology is paramount. Pursue search opportunities in industries in which your specialty area is a driver.

Avoid companies where everyone is an industry switcher. Outsiders can often bring a fresh perspective to a company's challenges. But a management team needs some industry experts to provide stability and grounding in reality. "Cross-industry transfers have to be confident enough to know an idea will work before they recommend it," says B. Merle Gilmore, a Wynnewood, Pennsylvania consultant who has worked in the transportation, health care, and consumer products industries. "Industry insiders have to validate whether a new idea is going to work in their unique setting."

Watch the clock. Move before becoming trapped by your compensation and 401(k) plan, or before you become typecast by your company or industry. "Generally, we recommend transplanting your talents if you have been with your organization more than four years without a promotion," says headhunter McCreary.

Recruiter Scorecard: Culture Fit

ENHANCERS

Recognition of cultural issues

Ability to compare/contrast your cultural background

Similar cultural background and management style as client's

DIMINISHERS

Lack of awareness of cultural issues

Dissimilar cultural background and management style

AND NEVER . . .

Insist that culture fit isn't important

16

LEADERSHIP PRESENCE PROFILE:

RICHARD H. BROWN, CEO, EDS

Invigoration personified

Recently named chairman and CEO of data processing giant Electronic Data Systems (EDS), Richard H. Brown is cut from a different mold than predecessors H. Ross Perot and Les Alberthal. The first outsider to take the top job in the company's thirty-six-year history, Brown was brought in to shake up the place, according to headhunter Gerry Roche, who recruited him from London-based Cable & Wireless. With a challenge of reviving the gung-ho spirit that Ross Perot created when he founded EDS back in the 1960s, Brown is charged with eradicating complacency and getting the company moving again. "The board is convinced he'll be able to recharge the place," says Roche. "Dick did a helluva job at Cable & Wireless, where the culture was even more entrenched than it is at EDS."

A MANDATE TO CHANGE

Once a subsidiary of General Motors, EDS is the world's second largest computer services firm. The company runs large mainframe systems and provides an array of computer and information technology outsourcing services to 9,000 clients, including Southland Corporation (owner of the 7-11 convenience chain), carmaker Saturn, and Britain's Rolls-Royce. With more than 119,000 employees worldwide, EDS also owns A.T. Kearney, the billion-dollar management consulting firm. However, the company has seen competitors like IBM and Computer Sciences Corporation chip away at its pre-eminent status as an independent computer management and services company. In 1998, EDS signed only one-third the number of service contracts that IBM did, and its revenue growth was less than half the industry average. According to Roche, EDS considered several candidates in its search for a new CEO after chairman Les Aberthal announced his retirement in 1998. "Dick didn't just have the credentials to get into the ballpark. What made him the ace pitcher were his personal characteristics—his executive presence and fit."

A PREFERENCE FOR ACTION

Although Brown looks like a standard-issue EDS executive—blue suit, white shirt—he was clearly hired to invigorate the company's sluggish culture. A few short weeks after showing up for work in January 1999, Brown made it obvious that things were going to change. "I like action," says Brown, fifty-one, a New Jersey native who served as chairman of one of Britain's biggest telecommunications companies for twenty-nine months. And if he repeats the tradition he started at his former company, EDS is in for plenty of it.

A twenty-eight-year veteran of the telecommunications industry, Brown is a ball of fire who knows how to shake up a company—and make people feel good about doing it. "His energy and animation are exceptional," says Roche. After joining Cable & Wireless in 1996, Brown moved 65 of the company's top 100 executives into new positions in less than two years. Twenty-five others quit. And Brown drove Cable & Wireless aggressively to acquire new businesses, ditch foundering operations, and shed its image as a lumbering holdover from Britain's colonial era. According to security analysts, Brown is likely to apply the same tonic to EDS. With an eye for strategic gaps and a proven ability to fill them with acquisitions that make sense, he may even explore the possibility of breaking off parts of EDS to grow at a faster rate. Says Howard Anderson, president of the Yankee Group, a market research firm based in Boston, "He may decide he wants to take more risks."

The MCI WorldCom deal is a cornerstone of Brown's dynamic approach to getting a business back on all fours. EDS and MCI WorldCom will swap $17 billion in assets and 13,000 employees to exchange network and computer services outsourcing. EDS will also buy MCI Systemhouse, a computer services unit, for $1.6 billion, and the two companies will explore how to jointly pursue new business and bid for major corporate data and networking contracts (MCI WorldCom will provide the network and EDS the data crunching and systems integration). Expected to lead to electronic business offerings like Internet-based banking and utility billing services, the alliance will open the door to new customers.

AN OUTSIDER'S CHALLENGE

Appointing someone like Brown, a reputed cost-cutter, is a classic tactic used by companies that desire a major culture shift. An outsider—particularly one with a record as strong as Brown's—is almost always more effective in sending a wakeup call to customers, employees, and stockholders than an insider, no matter how well-qualified. Brown successfully repositioned Cable & Wireless, Britain's number two telecommunications company, as an aggressive competitor by shuffling executives, acquiring new businesses, and ditching operations that he no longer wanted. Expanding the company's international reach with twenty-one deals valued at more than $20 billion, Brown bought companies in Australia and Panama and acquired MCI's Internet business.

Earlier, as CEO of Ameritech, he led a corporate restructuring that organized the company by product rather than geography. "Action changes a business," says Brown. "I'm looking for the right answer fast." And he's as good as his word. In the first six weeks on the job at EDS, he sued Xerox, one of EDS's largest customers, for breach of contract; moved Internet-based services to the top of EDS's priority list; and finalized the alliance with MCI WorldCom to access leading-edge network technology and deliver new e-business products.

DOWN-HOME STYLE

Like the other executives profiled in this book, Brown was born neither to wealth nor to the business world. The son of a salesman who became a high school math teacher, Brown had an uneventful childhood and showed an early propensity for working with people, serving as president of his fraternity at Ohio University. He began cultivating a down-home—some say Midwestern—personal style from the day he entered the telecommunications business in 1969. And though he's the CEO of one of the world's largest service companies, he continues to reach out to people at all levels. On the day he flew into Dallas to accept the EDS job, Brown had his hired car cruise some residential neighborhoods to view houses and invited the driver to join him for lunch before boarding the return flight. The driver, who discovered only later that his lunch partner was the chairman and CEO of one of the world's biggest companies, was dumbfounded.

With a leadership presence quotient as high as his aspirations for EDS, Brown is definitely CEO material, though of a different sort than EDS is used to.

Appearance. No surprise: he looks like an airline pilot—gray hair, tall, and fit. And like most CEOs, he's highly conscious of his appearance and how he comes across to others. For a recent photo in the *Dallas Morning News,* he fussed with the photographer about the camera angle, the light source, and how tight the shot was.

Poise. Brown is relaxed, alert, and prepared. Unlike many telecommunications executives, whose style tends to be parochial and inflexible, he adapts quickly to new environments. Before assuming the helm at Cable & Wireless, he had never been to Britain. He impressed the British company with his strong self-confidence, or superb acting skills, by telling them, "I'll be a good student. I'll immerse myself early on and meet with clients, employees, and key investors." Brown is well aware of the ceremonial impact he can lend as EDS's CEO. He regularly calls on customers in person and on the phone.

Focus and energy. A rapid-fire dealmaker and self-described workaholic, Brown is a demanding boss who pushes staffers to take action rather than ponder ideas too long. "I understand the value of a strategic plan, but too many times people labor over the strategy to get it picture perfect while faltering on the execution," he says. As CEO of Cable & Wireless, his very American drive and determination didn't waver in the face of traditional British reticence. "He wasn't afraid of applying the pressure," says a telecommunications industry observer. "He instilled the need to perform where it didn't exist."

Intellect. There's no question that Brown is intellectually qualified for the job, say recruiters and industry observers. A quick study, Brown learned Cable & Wireless's business fast, and says he promises to do the same at EDS. Although he said little in his first six weeks as CEO, he announced that he wants to win more contracts and reduce expenses. He plans to sketch a turnaround program for the company in April '99, less than three months after starting. And he doesn't value intellectual skills more highly than practical abilities. "I admire intelligence," says Brown, "but I believe the world has more smart people than effective people."

Passion. Says Jim Ross, an analyst with ABM/AMRO, "At Cable & Wireless, Brown was an inspirational manager. He gave people high targets to meet and was viewed with a certain amount of awe." Brown believes a bold, decisive management approach is critical to aligning employees with a company's strategy and desired culture.

Like most executives with a strong agenda, he's not a practitioner of management by committee. "Consensus is not my code," he says. He is also convinced of the need to make his standards plain. "Leaders get the behavior they tolerate," he says.

Communication skills. Until Brown arrived, EDS's computers were incapable of sending a message to all employees. The massive bureaucracy that settled in when employees by the thousands were added had segmented the company into dozens of strategic business units with disparate computer systems. One of Brown's first actions was to topple the chain-of-command communications channels that made it impossible to function as one company. To spread the word out about his priorities, he has been sending e-mail messages directly to all EDS employees. And employees feel comfortable responding: since January, he has received more than 1,000 e-mails—mostly words of encouragement and suggestions for improving the company. Brown is a skilled user of nonverbal signals as well. After pointedly commenting about the overhead expense associated with the company's huge corporate headquarters facilities and fleet of aircraft, Brown is disposing of two of six corporate jets and one of two helicopters. He eliminated reserved spots for executives in EDS's parking lot, saying that those who wanted to park close to the building should come to work early.

Charisma. In contrast to his predecessor, Les Alberthal, a Ross Perot lieutenant who was viewed by employees and customers as aloof, though technically brilliant, Brown aggressively reaches out to a variety of audiences—customers, employees, and stockholders— for feedback, input, and ideas. Observers say that he is optimistic and outgoing, excelling at making people feel good about decisions and moving forward—unlike some of his peers at other large technology companies. Brown has the ability to relate to a wide variety of people, and he connects well with top executives as well as factory workers.

Brown brings an intimate style to a work force desensitized by years of corporate speak. One e-mail message to all 119,000 employees of EDS in February began, "Well, it's early morning again. I happened to be thinking of you and thought it was time to drop you another note." And in his first week on the job, Brown appeared unannounced in the middle of the night to meet workers at a computer operations center. This personal approach is something that EDS employees haven't experienced in many years. Brown hopes it will help transform the bureaucracy that has stunted EDS's growth into a fast-moving, customer-savvy work force.

Culture fit. Brown was hired because he fits the culture of the future EDS: aggressive, lean, decisive, and action oriented. Brown's people-oriented management style contrasts dramatically with that of Alberthal. "From a style point of view, Brown acts like one of the team—not the guy at the top," says Paul McCartney, president of Technology Partners, a search firm specializing in recruiting telecommunications and high-tech executives. "He realizes how important it is to relate downward in an organization, as well as upward."

Career Timeline: Dick Brown

Education

Ohio University   B.S., Communications   1969

Business Experience

1999–current   Electronic Data Systems—Plano, Texas
                Chairman and CEO

1996–1998   Cable & Wireless—London
                CEO

1995–1996   H&R Block—Kansas City, Mo.
                President and CEO

1990–1995   Ameritech—Chicago
                Vice Chairman

1981–1990   United Telecommunications (later Sprint)
                Executive Vice President; Chief Information and
                Planning Officer

1969–1981   Ohio Bell
                Division Manager (last position held)

Boards

The Seagram Company
Pharmacia and Upjohn Inc.

17

LEADERSHIP PRESENCE AROUND THE WORLD

The demand for multicultural, multilingual management talent who can lead companies with global operations is skyrocketing. Sometimes Americans are best suited to handle the challenge.

The world's search for a new economic equilibrium has created an array of new opportunities for executives interested in working abroad. Western European unity, the evolution of Central and Eastern Europe, free trade in North America, and expansion in Latin America and the Pacific Rim are transforming relationships between countries. At the same time, these forces present demanding new challenges to businesses around the globe.

SCOOPING UP GLOBAL TALENT

Since 1992, when the European Common Market was dissolved, the pace of international executive recruiting has accelerated dramatically, and most major search firms have been conducting international assignments for a decade or more. As American companies expand overseas, they typically seek executives to manage their overseas operations. Similarly, European and Asian companies work closely with executive recruiters to find executives for their U.S. divisions. And the largest multinational companies are adopting a "best athlete" approach to leadership, scooping up talented executives from around the world.

Directing your career overseas is not simply a matter of sending your resume or waiting for an executive recruiter to call. It's often difficult for Americans to join foreign companies because most countries, particularly in Europe, discourage locally based companies from hiring foreigners for positions within their native country. Unless you have been sent abroad by a U.S. firm, it's almost impossible to obtain working papers. However, if you envision joining a major U.S. company and jetting off to a high-powered executive post in Paris, realize that one of the latest casualties of the re-engineering craze may be American executives with aspirations for working abroad.

Many search firms have experienced a fundamental shift in their U.S. clients' attitudes toward overseas staffing. In the late 1980s, companies planning to launch an operation in, for example, Germany, would simply select an executive from their U.S. management team and send him—rarely her—abroad. Today, their approach is radically different. Companies want to hire local executives. As American companies become more sophisticated about conducting business overseas, they have come to realize that there are significant cultural differences between the United States and Europe, Asia, or South

America, and between individual countries in those continents. They've learned, often the hard way, that working within the cultural context of each country is essential for business success.

MORE THAN JUST ETIQUETTE

Since the economic unification of Western Europe more than 14 years ago, American executives have been bombarded with advice on how to operate a successful business in a market with twelve countries, 360 million consumers, and significant potential. Most of this advice, however, has focused on shaking hands, presenting business cards, and other niceties of foreign etiquette.

To manage successfully in Europe, however, American companies and their executives need to know more than protocol. There are fundamental differences between American and European companies in corporate structure, management style, and employment law. Unless American executives understand these differences, they will have little chance of operating successfully abroad.

As a result of cultural traditions and political/economic disparities, management style—the manner in which an executive relates to employees and makes decisions—varies widely throughout Europe. In Europe, it is generally true that the farther north you go, the more participative the management style. It's often said that in Sweden, managers don't tell employees what to do, they convince them, and it's easier to find workers' councils and consensus management in Germany and Scandinavia than in Italy and Spain.

According to recruiter Don Utroska, who has conducted numerous transatlantic search assignments, corporate structure, generally legally mandated, can greatly influence a company's management style. In Germany, for example, management structure is tightly controlled by law. Corporations are run by management committees *(Geschaftsleitung)* whose members rotate top decision-making responsibility and have clear lines of command to appropriate employee groups within the company.

Executives in Germany tend to have extensive technical training and oftentimes higher degrees, especially in engineering-related businesses. Utroska, a partner with Chicago boutique Dieckmann & Associates, says German managers will rarely move out of their special field and will hold almost every management position within the relevant division or group before reaching the senior management level.

In France, most corporations are very much a one-person show, with a single *president-directeur* (PDG) holding both chairman and CEO responsibilities. PDGs are often graduates of the of the country's elite *grandes ecoles* (technical universities), and they are expected to be brilliant technical planners and adept at industry, finance, and government relations.

People skills, however, are often not part of their portfolio. French companies typically have management hierarchies that discourage informality and reinforce a sense of "us" and "them," leading to difficult labor relations—a constant in France.

British companies tend to be more similar to American organizations. They typically have a board of management that can be led by a non-operating chairman, while the company's actual operations are run by a managing director or CEO. Future managers are pinpointed at an early age and rotated through various departments in the company for a broad—but not always thorough—overview of operations. High-level British executives, however, often tend to be aloof and somewhat out of touch with their company's workers, according to Utroska. Often a wide gulf exists between management and labor, possibly a holdover from Britain's longstanding class system.

WHO'S RIGHT FOR THE JOB?

To motivate and manage their overseas work forces, American companies increasingly consider leadership presence in selecting an appropriate local executive or an expatriate U.S. executive for the post. Understanding the ethnic mix of the work force that will be managed is crucial, because certain national styles are more compatible than others. Swedes, for example, may be frustrated by French executives who don't believe in consensus management. Hierarchical Germans may not blend well with more emotional Italian executives. British executives are well respected for their financial and accounting expertise, but may not have the language capability to function effectively as general managers outside the United Kingdom. In some cases, the best solution may be an American with international management experience.

GLOBAL MANAGERS

To increase harmony among national cultures, some companies look for global managers who speak several different languages and are at home in a variety of cultures. Not surprisingly, these individuals are hard to find at all but the most senior levels. As an alternative, executives from Belgium, Holland, or Switzerland are considered good "blenders."

Other companies seek top American executives who have worked for large U.S. multinational companies because of their experience managing global companies. In an unprecedented move, SwissAir recently appointed American Airlines executive Jeff Katz as its new CEO. Katz is a veteran of deregulation, which the European airline industry will soon face. Dick Brown, an American telecommunications executive, was selected by British telecommunications company Cable & Wireless for his turnaround expertise.

PRODUCTIVITY VS. PLAYTIME

Although the standardizing that is taking place in European currencies may soon translate to other economic areas, maintaining a high level of productivity in the face of employee vacations and holidays is a challenge, even for the most seasoned European manager. Four to six weeks of vacation is typical and there are an average of twelve civic and religious holidays per year in most Western European countries. More employee downtime results from *Kur,* an additional seven- to ten-day, fully paid health retreat that is popular among German-speaking employees.

These frequent vacations and holidays, and the fact that they occur at different times all over Europe, can frustrate American companies that are used to a consistent, nonstop flow of business. Productivity-conscious Americans also can be frustrated by workday rituals that are commonplace throughout Europe.

In addition to a sixty- to ninety-minute lunch period and fifteen minutes of day-end clean-up time, employees—from plant workers to secretaries to executives—take twenty-minute morning and afternoon breaks, often with beer or wine. As a result, a nine-hour workday typically yields only seven hours of productive work.

U.S. executives are used to hiring and keeping employees based on their effectiveness and performance on the job. This is not necessarily the case in Europe, says Utroska. Everybody—from secretaries to CEOs—has a contract that virtually guarantees permanent employment, no matter what the company's financial condition or business objectives. Once individuals have been hired, it's not easy to fire them, no matter how bad their job performance.

WOMB TO TOMB

Dismissing an employee for poor performance is possible, but the costs can be significant. According to Utroska, several years ago a major American pharmaceutical company operating in Sweden attempted to fire an alcoholic employee who had not responded to treatment programs and other company-paid assistance. It took more than two years to get him off the payroll, during which time he came to work drunk, was incoherent by the end of the day, and annoyed other workers in the process.

In some socialist countries like France and Belgium, the only grounds for immediate dismissal are criminal behavior. Laying off employees following acquisitions, management changes, or restructuring—standard practice in the United States—is extremely difficult and rarely occurs.

To circumvent some of the problems caused by permanent employment, many European countries insist on a six-month trial period as part of the employment contract. Although lower-level workers generally accept this trial period, many executives refuse to do so. This can present a special problem in recruiting executives, who are understandably concerned about a guaranteed position before leaving their current job.

UNIQUELY AMERICAN ASPECTS OF LEADERSHIP PRESENCE

American companies should not expect European managers to adopt some uniquely American aspects of leadership presence. For example, Europeans have a hard time understanding the egalitarian culture of the U.S. corporate world. Although European workers have more rights than their American counterparts, they operate in a unionized environment where workers and management view each other as different species. Most European managers find the notion of "teamwork" difficult to grasp.

Certain icons of American management culture, such as pay for performance and commission salaries, are not well received in Europe. Many Europeans—particularly in the south—value highly subjective factors like loyalty, perseverance, and process and can be insulted by "objective" measurement and reward systems based on the bottom line.

LEADERSHIP PRESENCE ESSENTIALS

The ability to communicate in another language is the first step to building leadership presence abroad. While fluency isn't essential, learning another language well enough to converse socially demonstrates interest, commitment, and emotional intelligence. Although English is certainly the language of international business, U.S. executives who speak the language of the country where they do business and make an effort to adopt its cultural traditions can make a far greater impact. However, a recent survey found that fewer than 25 percent of American CEOs are fluent in any foreign language. And only a tiny percentage spoke any Asian languages, considered the most vital for the twenty-first century.

If your native language is Mandarin, Cantonese, or Spanish and you can communicate reasonably well in English, you may be an ideal candidate for an overseas management position with an American company. Local languages are far more important for effective management in markets abroad, and many U.S. companies are "getting over" their tendency to hire the best English speaker—rather than the best manager—for a foreign management post.

Nationality. U.S. companies have realized that transferring an American to run a foreign office, particularly an American without any language skills, is a recipe for disaster. Aside from the expense of expatriating an executive and his or her family, the executive presence issues are compelling: without an intimate knowledge of the local culture, business customs, and expected management style, an American executive can rarely represent the company as well as a local executive.

Experience. As in the United States, business qualifications and resume factors are only part of the requirements needed to perform successfully as an executive. In addition to the language and nationality issues, knowledge of the country and a sensitivity to its cultural heritage and management etiquette are essential.

Rapport. While e-mail and telecommunications makes it easy for executives around the world to stay in close touch regardless of location, technology isn't enough when a business relationship must be built across a thousand-mile gap. When two executives see each other only a few times a year, their rapport and consistent thinking must enable them to anticipate the other's thinking style and decision-making process. At Pepsico, for example, CEO Wayne Calloway interviews every candidate for the top 600 jobs in the company. His rationale? Whether they work in Paris or Pakistan, they have the chance to get to know each other and make sure they have the same values, objectives, and standards in mind.

THE MARKET FOR EXPATRIATES

Despite these considerations, there is certainly a market for expatriate executives. As the global work force has become more mobile, worldwide corporations now cross borders to recruit outstanding executives in increasing numbers. Major areas of interest among American and global corporations are:

Global Managers. With the consolidation of the Western European economies and the continued growth of the Pacific Rim countries, recruiters predict strong demand for executives, in almost every industry, with international management experience. "Right now, the largest pool of global management talent works in U.S. multinationals," says Utroska. "German, French, and Swiss companies are recruiting from Citibank, Morgan, and other international companies that have been practicing global management for years."

Pan-Continent Executives. Often called Euroexecutives, these management hybrids have experience running multi-country operations. With exposure to a variety of cultures and excellent language skills, they are capable of developing a continent-wide strategy with local tactics for each European nation. As we enter the twenty-first century, Pan-Asian and Pan-Latin American executives will be in demand as well.

Strategic Planning. This will be a top staff career in the twenty-first century, and individuals who are capable of dealing with multiple European cultures will be in particular demand.

Manufacturing. As corporations worldwide focus on quality, they increasingly seek executives with expertise in total quality management, statistical process control, and just-in-time inventory management programs.

Human Resources. As demographic changes, attitudes toward work, employee retention, and flex programs become key issues worldwide, human resource executives will assume greater responsibilities—and become harder to find.

The Environment. Environmental experts will become increasingly responsible for managing not only disposal but also utilization, recycling, and re-use for manufactured products as well as energy and fuel products.

To indicate your availability and capability for an international posting, let it be known that you have language skills. Or that you are traveling abroad in your free time. Another way is by demonstrating competence in dealing with ethnic cultures in the domestic market. Many companies in California, the Southwest, southern Florida, or New York deal with large customer bases that are largely immigrant or non-English speaking. Working in ethnic marketing or an associated field can help you demonstrate and build competencies in working with cultures other than your own.
RODERICK C. GOW, EXECUTIVE VICE PRESIDENT,
LAI WORLDWIDE

FOUR PATHS TO A CAREER ABROAD

If you have aspirations for a senior executive position over-seas, investigate four major pathways for expanding your career globally:

- If you already work for a global organization, make it clear that you are interested in an overseas assign-ment. If you plan to change companies, seek out those that operate one or more overseas offices, even if the job doesn't initially involve any travel.

- Join a large U.S. company that has a significant per-centage of overseas business, like a consumer pack-age goods corporation, or a company in an industry that is rapidly expanding abroad, like a computer or software organization. Although it's likely your new company will hire local nationals to manage over-seas offices, you may be able to join a transition group that sets up a new overseas operation and later segue into a full-time position.

- Join the U.S. division of a global company head-quartered in Europe or another area. Many foreign companies actively promote their outstanding U.S. executives to other positions around the world.

- Join an international professional services firm in consulting, accounting, or investment banking. The largest firms typically have several offices around the world, and your chances of being reassigned are sig-nificantly greater than in a conventional industrial company.

18

LEADERSHIP
PRESENCE: 2010

Today's knowledge workers have a much greater shot at the top spot—if they can think strategically, motivate people, and look and act like leaders.

What will a manager need to be a successful leader in tomorrow's business world? Take a look at the following profiles:

Greg Brenneman, thirty-five, CEO of Continental Airlines, is a Mennonite wonder boy who at age thirty-four helped turn an ailing airline into a high-flying outfit. An analytical whiz who's also a people person, Brenneman has helped the company's stock rise nearly ninefold in his first eighteen months on the job. Leadership presence? Energy: few can keep up with Brenneman, who sleeps an average of four hours a night, starts his workday at 5 A.M., and spends 75 percent of his time traveling, much of it abroad. A sense of urgency: "I love making a difference," he says, "and doing it quickly." And a personal touch: a recent internal memo ended on a high note: "Yesterday was a good day! Our stock closed at $60 3/8 and I picked up my '64 'Vette."

Catherine Hapka, forty-two, went from taming a bunch of union workers at a Schlitz brewery to overseeing a $6.8 billion telecommunications business for US West. Her stated goal: to "raise the temperature in the room." Leadership presence? Lead sentences: "What's the headline?" she demands when confronted with insufficiently digested data. "My job is to get us ready for brutal competition," she explains. "No one believes a Baby Bell can be a lean, mean machine." Passion: "I love to do things that people say can't be done," she says with a grin. People skills: tries to involve workers in big ideas that matter to the survival of the company rather than small processes.

Art Collins, forty-eight, is chief operating officer of Medtronic, a $1.7 billion manufacturer of medical devices. Leadership presence? "You can't manage from behind a desk" is Collins's motto, and he regularly makes the rounds of hospitals and factory floors to inspect what he expects, see his products in action, and hear firsthand from customers about what Medtronic can do better.

These executives and a host of corporate America's up-and-coming leaders demonstrate the new reality of today's business world: no matter how strong your business credentials and solid your achievements, they're only the minimum requirement for gaining an executive level job. You can have a Harvard MBA, intellectual brilliance, and a history of successful projects. You can have the right job at the right time with the right boss. All of these "resume factors" will likely gain you access to a solid management position. But without leadership presence, you aren't likely to be successful in a top job—in your current company or a new organization.

TODAY'S KNOWLEDGE WORKER

Most of the executives recruited by headhunters for top corporate executives are between ages forty and sixty— people born between 1939 and 1959. But as information-based products and services increasingly drive the U.S. economy, the demographic profile of tomorrow's CEO is changing. Everyone knows about the twenty-seven-year-old kids running million dollar computer companies. What they may not be aware of is the rising generation of young executives whose computer literacy, line management experience, and people skills are propelling them ahead at mainline manufacturing and service organizations. With every industry—from steel making to telecommunications—driven more and more by technological change, today's knowledge worker has a much greater shot at a top spot if he or she can think strategically, motivate people, and look and act like a leader. Says recruiter Jeffrey Christian, "Twenty-first-century CEOs will be netcentric—if they're not, they will lose a lot of business."

It's not only recruiters who realize that some of the basic leadership presence factors like appearance and poise are less important in the computer industry. How you look and which fork you use became inconsequential a decade ago, according to many headhunters. Says Anne Peckenpaugh, a recruiter with Schweichler and Associates who conducts many searches for Silicon Valley companies, "Sometimes the geekier you are, the better." She points to John Morgridge, president of Cisco Sytems. "By the conventional rules of leadership presence, he doesn't appear to have it. He wears brown suits and looks like a fuddy duddy."

TRANSCENDING THE GEEK ROLE

As corporate America becomes increasingly netcentric, certain leadership presence standards may become relaxed. But, say most recruiters, don't hold your breath. Even though Morgridge may not look the part, he has all of the other key leadership presence factors solidly in place. "He is an effective leader because he has the technical know-how, the communications skills, and the people smarts," says Peckenpaugh. "Bill Gates is also nerdy but he's an articulate visionary—when you talk to him, you feel something is happening. You're both sitting down but your brains are going 90 miles per hour." And despite their predilection for brown suits and rumpled clothes, most of the computer geniuses know when to spruce themselves up. Says a recruiter who works extensively with IPO companies, "The fact is, when these startup guys want to go public or get some financing, they go to Wall Street dressed in a navy suit."

A recent search illustrates how essential leadership presence is. A major technology company was evaluating two external candidates for its top executive position. Both finalists were impressive on paper, technically sophisticated, and able to talk the game. The first, an electrical engineer, had the brains, skills, and technological know-how to chart a complex path to market leadership. However, it wasn't clear that he would be able to transcend his "computer guru" role and relate successfully to non-technical constituencies. In contrast, the candidate who was ultimately selected combined top-level technical savvy, a partnerlike approach to managing, and international experience. His effectiveness with colleagues as well as clients earned him the CEO slot at the company, whose market value has risen 150 percent since his arrival in 1997.

STARTUP COMPANIES

As entrepreneurs and startup companies proliferate, leadership presence is taking a new twist, according to David Beirne of Benchmark Capital, a recruiting firm specializing in venture-backed businesses and startups. "If you plan on joining a startup, you must be able to change direction and turn on a dime," says Beirne. "Willingness to accept change and implement new strategies as the company's initiatives change will be the key to your success—and the company's." According to Beirne, the majority of executives making the switch into this type of environment are coming from a larger corporate culture where support professionals are in abundance. However, when they join a startup, they have to swallow their pride very quickly. "If composing your own correspondence or e-mail and making your own sandwich is beneath you, don't cross over to this side," he adds.

ACTING LIKE THE CEO

Most ambitious executives will not build their careers in Silicon Valley, where dressing casual and looking nerdy can enhance your prospects. In corporate America, say recruiters, if you want to become a CEO you need to look, talk, act, and think like a CEO. While the leadership presence standards for appearance and poise may be shifting a

few degrees, it's not worth taking the chance. Says recruiter
Gerry Roche, "Always dress one level above."

> *A CEO in the twenty-first century must have enough
> smarts to see his or her business from the 50,000 foot level,
> enough experience to manage the details as well as the big
> picture, enough personal confidence to get excited about what
> they do, and tolerate ambiguity at the same time.*
> JOHN THOMPSON, VICE-CHAIRMAN,
> HEIDRICK & STRUGGLES

LEADERSHIP PRESENCE FACTORS FOR THE TWENTY-FIRST CENTURY

To convince recruiters and their client's board of directors
that you have the operating skills to operate in a twenty-
first-century environment, you must have a global intellect
and a great deal of personal flexibility. You must demonstrate the ability to influence, adjust to rapidly changing
business models, manage change, and keep many balls in
the air simultaneously. In addition, you will be judged on
the eight fundamentals of leadership presence.

Intellect. An executive's ability to see an issue, decision,
or opportunity in a larger context and view it from many
perspectives will continue to be a crucial factor in his or her
leadership presence in the twenty-first century. Corporate
America has produced many effective tacticians. However,
the ability to think and manage strategically is what truly
distinguishes leaders from administrators. By building a
vision of what business the organization should be, identifying its strengths and opportunities, positioning it effectively against competition, and structuring it to reach its

maximum potential, strategists such as Bob Kidder (Borden), Harvey Golub (American Express), and Lou Gerstner (IBM) demonstrate the "vision thing" required of top leaders.

Technology savvy. Knowing how information technology can be leveraged to support company strategy and decision-making is also essential for today's executive. Leaders must understand the role computers play in shaping their current markets and operations, the potential technology has for improving their processes and products, and how it can help them position effectively against competition. A warning: don't become so preoccupied with technology that you lose sight of the "big picture" and the importance of human inter-action. Charles Wong, CEO of Computer Associates, cautions that reliance on e-mail can depersonalize organizations and overwhelm managers with unnecessary detail. At his organization, e-mail is forbidden and executives are expected to walk down the hall to communicate person to person.

Passion. Just like leaders today, twenty-first-century CEOs and senior-level executives will want a top-level management job, and want it badly. As Catherine Hapka of US West says, "My goal is to be CEO of a major corporation. Period. Ambition is good for the people who hire me, good for the people who follow me. I don't know why people are so worried about talking about ambition. It's what drives this country."

Focus. With the proliferation of new products, markets, and technologies, focus will be even more important for the next generation of executives.

Communication skills. Tomorrow's executives will be skilled at simplifying the complex, reducing a complicated concept or maneuver to a one-page chart, and presenting an idea, issue, or directive with simplicity, humor, and sincerity.

Appearance and poise. As the economy booms, executives have extra cash to spend on top quality clothes and grooming. They're entertaining clients, venture capitalists, and others more often over lunch or dinner. According to Judith Re, an etiquette consultant who has cured many corporate executives of bad table manners, "They want to make sure they're putting their best foot forward." Many executives at a variety of companies, including software producers, now use the services of image consultants or etiquette coaches to polish the veneer, lest it detract from the substance underneath.

Charisma. Says Steve Mader, managing director of Christian & Timbers's Boston practice, "A key element for success will be the ability to win people over to your side, to be an opinion leader. Selling ideas and getting people on board—employees, customers, Wall Street—is for every top executive. Today, it's the most important job of a top executive."

Culture fit. Like their predecessors, twenty-first-century executives will be focused on more than just the bottom line: they have a keen sense of their organization's values, operational behaviors, and attitudes about change, and recognize these factors as they move their agenda into place in the organization. Using this framework, they must create a clear purpose and direction for an organization. And they must align all corporate systems with that direction for a sustained period and build organizational commitment to common goals.

SIX MUST-HAVES FOR TOMORROW'S LEADERS

Almost every leadership authority has written on this subject with illumination and depth. But the people who will actually round up and place tomorrow's leaders—executive recruiters—say that their clients are increasingly seeking six characteristics in their future leaders:

- *Flexibility:* An ability to adapt to ever-changing demands, whether it's taking a big risk on a new technology or reviving loyalty in a dispirited work force.
- *Consensus orientation:* Favoring a style that's participatory rather than autocratic.
- *MBA:* It's not merely an empty credential—it does provide an edge in business.
- *People savvy:* Most of tomorrow's executives will view relationships with people as the foundation for progress. They've honed their people skills and are competent managers of human feeling and behavior.
- *Global outlook:* Substantial foreign experience will be a hallmark of tomorrow's managers. Twenty-first-century managers view their home country as nothing more than one region in a global marketplace. They understand how key cultural differences are in business plans and organizations. An overseas assignment is no longer considered a backwater but rather a fast track to the top.
- *Exposure to corporate governance:* Boardroom experience is a critical landmark on the development path of any executive aiming for a leadership role. Whether they serve on their own organization's

board, another company's board, or the board of a high-powered, not-for-profit organization, future leaders will deal with key strategic issues like the financial health of the organization, its mission and vision, and the impact of strategy on key constituencies, including shareholders.

19

EXECUTIVES
WITH PRESENCE

America's top executive recruiters nominated the following 161 executives for their exceptional leadership presence.

William Adams
President, Bucknell University

William E. Ardell
President and CEO, Southam
   Inc.

Gideon Argov
Chairman of the Board,
   President and CEO,
   Kollmorgen

C. Michael Armstrong
Chairman and CEO, AT&T

John H. Atterbury III
President and CEO, SBC
   International, SBC
   Communications Inc.

Michael E. Barker
Partner, T.L. Ventures

Donald D. Belcher
Chairman, President and CEO,
   Banta Corporation

Phillip Bennett
CEO, Renfro Group Lt.

Mark Bertolini
Retired Executive Vice
   President, Nylcare Health
   Plans Inc.

Jeffrey P. Bezos
Founder and CEO,
   Amazon.com

Theresa A. Bischoff
President, New York University Hospitals Center and Executive Vice President, Mount Sinai–NYU Medical Center and Health System

Norman P. Blake Jr.
Chairman, President and CEO, Promus Hotel Corp.

John B. Blystone
CEO, SPX

Dan Boggan Jr.
Chief Operating Officer, NCAA

Stephen F. Bollenbach
President and CEO, Hilton Hotels Corp.

Michael R. Bonsignore
CEO, Honeywell Inc.

John D. Borgia
Executive Vice President of Human Resources, Joseph E. Seagram & Sons Inc.

Peter Brabeck-Letmathe
CEO, Nestle S.A.

Alan Brass
President and CEO, Promedica Health System Inc.

Eli Broad
Chairman, SunAmerica

Dennis Brown
President and CEO, Pinkerton Inc.

Richard H. Brown
Chairman and CEO, EDS

Warren E. Buffett
Chairman and CEO, Berkshire Hathaway Inc.

Alan Cantrell
Vice President of Enterprise Solutions, Compuware

Marshall N. Carter
Chairman and CEO, State Street Bank and Trust Co.

Elaine L. Chao
Distinguished Fellow, The Heritage Foundation

Thomas F. Chapman
President and CEO, Equifax Inc.

Paul R. Charron
Chairman and CEO, Liz Claiborne Inc.

Kenneth I. Chenault
President and Chief Operating Officer, American Express Company

Stephen D. Chesebro
President and CEO,
    PennzEnergy

Michael Cimet
Strategic Business Unit
    President, Latin America,
    EDS

Bruce L. Claflin
President and COO, 3Com
    Corporation

Joseph B. Costello
Vice Chairman, Knowledge
    Universe

Christos Cotsakos
Chairman and CEO, E★TRADE
    Group Inc.

Joy Covey
Chief Financial Officer,
    Amazon.com

Gary Crittenden
Senior Vice President and Chief
    Financial Officer, Monsanto
    Company

Sally Cunningham
Vice President, Corporate
    Human Resources and
    Administration, Warner-
    Lambert Co.

Michael Dell
Chairman and CEO, Dell
    Computer Corporation

Bruce Evans
General Partner, Summit
    Partners

Bob Fabbio
Partner, T.L. Ventures

Mikel D. Faulkner
Chairman and CEO, Harken
    Energy Corporation

Daniel R. Feehan
President, Cash America
    International Corporation

Tim Ferguson
Chief Investment Officer,
    Putnam Investments

Frank M. Fischer
Chairman, Heartport Inc.

James E. Fligg
Senior Vice President, Strategic
    Planning, BP Amoco PLC

David Fuente
Chairman and CEO, Office
    Depot Inc.

Robert G. Funari
President and CEO, Syncor
    International Corporation

Clarence J. Gabriel Jr.
President, Corporate Express
Delivery Systems

Bill Gates
Chairman and CEO, Microsoft
Corporation

William W. George
Chairman and CEO, Medtronic
Inc.

Louis V. Gerstner Jr.
Chairman and CEO, IBM

Raymond V. Gilmartin
Chairman, President and CEO,
Merck & Co. Inc.

E. V. "Rick" Goings
Chairman and CEO,
Tupperware

Patricia Graham
President, Spencer Foundation

Carl Grivner
CEO, Western Hemisphere
Cable and Wireless

Gary C. Grom
Senior Vice President, Human
Resources, Sara Lee
Corporation

Andrew S. Grove
Chairman, Intel Corporation

Richard Gural, Ph.D.
Vice President, Drug Regulatory
Affairs, Sanofi
Pharmaceuticals Inc.

David Hale
President and CEO, Women
First HealthCare Inc.

Jim Hardymon
Retired chairman, Textron Inc.

William Hargett
Senior Vice President, Santa Fe
Snyden, Snyder Oil
Corporation

Tom Hicks
CEO, Hicks, Muse, Tate & Furst
Inc.

W. August Hillenbrand
President and CEO,
Hillenbrand Industries

Dick Holbrook
President and Chief Operating
Officer, AFC Enterprises

James Hyman
President and Managing
Director, GE Capital
Modular Space

Douglas Ivester
Chairman and CEO, Coca-Cola
Company

Kevin Jenkins
President and CEO, The
  Westaim Corporation

Peter Johnson
President and CEO, Agouron
  Pharmaceuticals Inc.

Robert Johnson
Chairman and CEO, Bowne and
  Co. Inc.

Paul Jones
Chairman, President and CEO,
  U.S. Can Corporation

David B. Kallis
Vice President,
  Communications, IBM
  Corporation

Glenn Kalnasy
President, Northern Group Inc.

Sussannah Kelly
Vice President, Human
  Resources, Merisel North
  America Inc.

Dan Keshian
President and CEO, Webline
  Communications
  Corporation

Leo Kiely
President and Chief Operating
  Officer, Coors Brewing Co.

Charles D. Kissner
Chairman and CEO, Digital
  Microwave Corporation

Arvind Korde
Vice President and General
  Manager, TRW

Fred Krehbiel
Chairman and CEO, Molex Inc.

Roman Kulich
President and CEO, SelectCare

Raymond J. Lane
President and Chief Operating
  Officer, Oracle Corporation

Dick Lappin
Former President, Fruit of the
  Loom

Geraldine Laybourne
Chairman and CEO, Oxygen
  Media

Charles R. Lee
Chairman and CEO, GTE

James B. Leer
Executive Vice President and
  Vice Chairman, Chase
  Manhattan Bank

Edward M. Liddy
Chairman, President and CEO,
  Allstate Corporation
  CEO, efdex, Inc.

Steve Lindseth
President and CEO,
    Complient, Inc.

Bob MacNally
Former President and
    Chairman, Tommy Armour
    Golf Co.

Phil Marineau
President and CEO, Pepsi-Cola
    North America

Ellen Marram
Former CEO, Tropicana
    Beverage

Robert Martin
President, Deutsche Financial
    Services

Arthur C. Martinez
Chairman and CEO, Sears,
    Roebuck & Co.

John S. McFarlane
President, Network Service
    Provider, Sun Microsystems

Robert J. McGee
Chairman and CEO, KBK
    Capital Corporation

Scott McNealy
Chairman, President and CEO,
    Sun Microsystems

Dana Mead
Chairman and CEO, Tenneco
    Inc.

Paul M. Meister
Vice Chairman, Executive Vice
    President and Chief Financial
    Officer, Fisher Scientific

John Meriwether
CEO, Long Term Capital
    Management

Bruce Miller
Senior Vice President,
    Northwestern Mutual Life
    Insurance Company

Heidi Miller
Chief Financial Officer,
    Citigroup

Charles R. Morgan
Executive Vice President and
    General Counsel, BellSouth
    Corporation

Gerard Moufflet
Senior Vice President and
    Managing Director, Advent
    International

Elisabeth S. Muhlenfeld
President, Sweet Briar College

Donal Mullen
Senior Managing Director, Bear
    Stearns & Company

Leo F. Mullin
President and CEO, Delta Airlines

Jim Mulva
Phillips Petroleum

Stephen Munger
Managing Director, Morgan Stanley Dean Witter

Joseph P. Nacchio
President and CEO, Qwest Communications

Henry Nasella
President and CEO, Online Retail Partners

George Nebel
President and CEO, Gemini Industries Inc.

Jonathon Newcomb
Chairman and CEO, Simon & Schuster Inc.

Lucio A. Noto
Chairman and CEO, Mobil Corporation

Dr. Ricardo Ochoa
Director of Pathology, Pfizer

Thomas E. Palmer
Vice President, Secretary and General Counsel, Mead Corporation

William P. Payne (Billy)
Ex-president of 1996 Atlanta Olympics

Eckhard Pfeiffer
President and CEO, Compaq Computer Corporation

Alfred Piergallini
Vice Chairman, President and CEO, Gerber Products Company

Lewis E. Platt
President, Kendall-Jackson Wines

John Polumbo
President and Chief Operating Officer, Excite Inc.

Ken Potashner
Chairman, President and CEO, S3 Inc.

Steve Puckett
President and CEO, MedCath Inc.

Philip J. Purcell
Chairman and CEO, Morgan Stanley Dean Witter

Richard Rainwater
Entrepreneur

Barry Rand
Chairman and CEO, Avis Rent
A Car Systems

John Rau
President and CEO, Chicago
Title Corporation

Edward T. Reilly
President and CEO, Big Flower
Holdings Inc.

John Richards
President, Starbucks

Tim Ring
Group President, C.R. Bard

Ellen Robinson
Senior Vice President,
Communications and
Government Affairs, Case
Corporation

David Rodriguez
Senior Vice President, Staffing
and Development, Marriott
International

Patricia F. Russo
Executive Vice President,
Corporate Staff Operations,
Lucent Technologies Inc.

Larry Sanders
President and CEO, Fujitsu
Computer Products of
America

William D. Sanders
Chairman and CEO, Security
Capital Group

Ron Sargent
President and Chief Operating
Officer, Staples, Inc.

Frank Savage
Chairman, Alliance Capital

Steve Schmidt
President and CEO, A.D.
Neilsen

Robert Schoenberger
Chairman and CEO, UNITIL
Corporation

Robert L. Seelert
Chairman, Saatchi & Saatchi

James Seiler
CEO, Mariner Systems Inc.

Alan G. Spoon
President and Chief Operating
Officer, Washington Post
Company

John Stanton
Chairman and CEO, Western
Wireless Corporation

Seymour Sternberg
Chairman, President and CEO,
New York Life Insurance
Company

John Stevenson
Vice President, Information
Management, Bristol-Myers
Squibb, Worldwide
Pharmaceuticals Division

Robert Strauss
President and CEO, Noven
Pharmaceuticals

John Thain
President and Co-Chief
Operating Officer, Goldman
Sachs & Company

Mort Topfer
Vice Chairman, Dell Computer
Corporation

John Trani
Chairman and CEO, Stanley
Works

Peter Ueberroth
CEO, Ambassadors Performance
Group Inc.

James Vincent
Chairman and CEO, Biogen
Inc.

David Wagner
CEO, Old Kent Bank

Julie Wainwright
CEO, Pets.com

Theodore Waitt
Chairman and CEO, Gateway
2000 Inc.

Martin D. Walker
Chairman and CEO, M.A.
Hanna Company

Henry Wendt
Retired CEO, SmithKline
Beecham

Lawrence Weinbach
Chairman, President and CEO,
Unisys Corporation

Jack Welch
Chairman and CEO, General
Electric Company

Sheelagh Whittaker
President and CEO, EDS
Canada

David Whatwas
Chairman and CEO, Whirlpool
Corporation

Philip Williamson
Vice Chairman and CEO,
  Williamson-Dickie
  Manufacturing Company

Vincent Wong
CEO, Queens Physicians Group

Robert C. Wright
President and CEO, NBC

Michael Yeager
Managing Director, Exxon
  Mobil

PARTICIPATING EXECUTIVE SEARCH CONSULTANTS

Donald T. Allerton, Allerton Heneghan & O'Neill.
Jacques P. Andre, Ray & Berndtson.
Donald P. Baiocchi, DP Baiocchi Associates.
Stephen A. Balogh, David Powell, Inc.
Gary R. Barton, Barton Associates.
Bruce M. Bastoky, January Management Group, Inc.
Martin H. Bauman, Martin H. Bauman Associates, Inc.
Robert E. Beaudine, Eastman & Beaudine Inc.
Dr. Joy Reed Belt, Joy Reed Belt Search Consultants.
John R. Berry II, Heidrick & Struggles.
Linda C. Bialecki, Bialecki, Inc.
Susan Bishop, Bishop Partners.
Gerald J. Bump, D.E. Foster Partners Inc.
C. Douglas Caldwell, LAI Ward Howell.
Robert M. Callan, Callan Associates, Ltd.
Pat Campbell, The Onstott Group.
Roy L. Caple, Ray & Berndtson.
Dennis M. Carey, Spencer Stuart.

Jeffrey E. Christian, Christian & Timbers.

William M. Cicchino, LAI Ward Howell.

John R. Clarey, Partner, Clarey & Andrews, Inc.

Donald B. Clark, Ray & Berndtson.

J. Robert Clarke, Furst Group/MPI.

Joseph W. Colavito II, LAI Ward Howell.

Bonnie Crabtree, Korn/Ferry International.

Peter D. Crist, Crist Partners.

Richard J. Cronin, SPHR/Hodge-Cronin & Associates, Inc.

Steven M. Darter, People Management Northeast.

David M. DeWilde, Chartwell Partners International.

Paul M. DiMarchi, DiMarchi Partners.

John P. Doyle, Ray & Berndtson.

Peter Dromeshauser, Dromeshauser Associates.

Peter Drummond-Hay, Russell Reynolds Associates.

Donald R. Duckworth, Horton International.

Craig J. Dudley, Ray & Berndtson.

Craig Dunlevie, Korn/Ferry International.

Bert H. Early, Early Cochran & Olson.

John G. Farish, Russell Reynolds Associates.

Leon A. Farley, Leon A. Farley Associates.

John R. Ferneborg, Ferneborg & Associates.

Kathryn A. Foreman, Korn/Ferry International.

Amanda C. Fox, Spencer Stuart.

David L. Gabriel, The Arcus Group.

Jay Gaines, Jay Gaines & Company.

Nicholas P. Gardiner, Gardiner & Townsend.

Debra S. Germaine, Fenwick Partners.

Carl Gilchrist, Spencer Stuart.

Trina D. Gordon, Boyden.

William E. Gould, Gould, McCoy & Chadick.

Peter G. Grimm, Nordemann Grimm.

Jordan M. Hadelman, Witt/Kieffer, Ford, Hadelman & Lloyd.

David O. Harbert, Sweeney, Harbert & Mummert.

Richard L. Hardison, Hardison & Company.

John Hawkins, Russell Reynolds Associates.

Paul Hawkinson, The Fordyce Letter.

Linda H. Heagy, Heidrick & Struggles.

Richard L. Hertan, Executive Manning Corporation.

David H. Hoffman, DHR International.

Jonathan S. Holman, The Holman Group.

Sidney A. Humphries, Korn/Ferry International.

Chris Hunt, Hunt-Scanlon Publishing.

Durant A. Hunter, Pendleton James and Associates.

W. Jerry Hyde, Hyde Danforth Wold & Co.

John Isaacson, Isaacson, Miller.

Kathleen A. Johnson, Barton Associates.

Howard L. Karr, Howard Karr & Associates.

Roger M. Kenny, Boardroom Consultants.

Richard E. Kinser, Kinser & Associates.

Lawrence S. Klock, Russell Reynolds Associates.

Gary Knisely, Accord Group/Johnson Smith & Knisely.

Richard F. Larsen, Larsen, Whitney, Blecksmith & Zilliacus.

David R. Lauderback, A.T. Kearney.

Helga Long, Horton International.

Steven Mader, Christian & Timbers.

John G. Martin, J3.

Neal L. Maslan, LAI Ward Howell.

Bill Matthews, Heidrick & Struggles.

Paul J. McCartney, Technology Partners, Ltd.

Joseph McCool, Executive Recruiter News.

Horacio McCoy, Korn/Ferry International.

Millington F. McCoy, Gould, McCoy & Chadick.

Chip McCreary, Austin-McGregor International.

Paul D. McKinnis, Korn/Ferry International.

James F. McSherry, Battalia Winston International.

Terry McSherry, TASA Worldwide/Johnson, Smith & Knisely Accord.

John T. Mestepey, A.T. Kearney.

Herbert Mines, Herbert Mines Associates.

P. John Mirtz, Mirtz Morice.

John T. Mitchell, Spencer Stuart.

Norman F. Mitchell, A.T.

Kearney. Rod Monahan, D.E.Foster Partners Inc.

James M. Montgomery, Houze, Shourds & Montgomery.

Edwin S. Mruk, Mruk & Partners.

P. Clarke Murphy, Russell Reynolds Associates.

Richard J. Nadzam, Nadzam, Lusk & Associates.

Todd Noebel, The Noebel Search Group, Inc.

Dayton Ogden, Spencer Stuart.

Thomas H. Ogdon, The Ogdon Partnership.

Andrew A. Olsen, A.T. Kearney.

Joseph Onstott, The Onstott Group.

Ted A. Orner, Russell Reynolds Associates.

Merle W. Owens, Merle Owens & Associates.

Frank Palma, Goodrich & Sherwood.

David W. Palmlund III, LAI Ward Howell.

Bernadette Pawlik, Pawlik/Dorman Partners.

Robert Pearson, LAI Ward Howell.

David R. Peasback, Canny, Bowen.

Nicholas J. Pierce, Heidrick & Struggles.

John Plummer, Plummer & Associates.

Charles A. Polachi Jr., Fenwick Partners.

Gary J. Posner, Educational Management Network.

David E. Preng, Preng & Associates Inc.

Conrad E. Prusak, Ethos Consulting.

Roger Quick, Norman Broadbent International.

David B. Radden.

Mary Jane Range, Bishop Partners.

Andrea Redmond, Russell Reynolds Associates.

Paul R. Ray Jr., Ray & Berndtson.

John H. Reynolds, Brissenden, McFarland, Fucella and Reynolds.

Russell Reynolds, Directorship.

Smooch Reynolds, The Repovich Reynolds Group.

Kenneth M. Rich, Ray & Berndtson.

Norman C. Roberts, Norman Roberts & Associates.

Nancy R. Roblin, Paul-Tittle Associates.

Gerard R. Roche, Heidrick & Struggles.

William D. Rowe III, D.E. Foster Partners Inc.

Scott Scanlon, Hunt-Scanlon Publishing.

Paul Schmidt, LAI Ward Howell.

Ann Peckenpaugh, Schweichler Associates.

Stephen R. Scroggins, Russell Reynolds Associates.

Steven A. Seiden, Seiden Associates.

Daniel M. Shepherd, Shepherd Bueschel & Provus.

Mel Shulman, McFeely Wackerle Shulman.

Fred Siegel, Conex Incorporated.

Patricia Sklar, Sklar & Associates.

Skott B. Burkland, Skott/Edwards Consultants.

Richard C. Slayton, Slayton International.

Herman M. Smith, Herman Smith Executive Initiatives.

Richard Sparbaro, EMA Partners.

Charles Splaine, Splaine & Associates.

Robert D. Spriggs, Spriggs & Company.

Gilbert R. Stenholm Jr., Spencer Stuart.

Ken G. Stevens, The Stevens Group.

Brian M. Sullivan, Sullivan & Company.

Charles W. Sweet, A.T. Kearney.

Carlton W. Thompson, Spencer Stuart.

John T. Thompson, Heidrick & Struggles.

J. Larry Tyler, Tyler & Company.

Donald R. Utroska, Dieckmann & Associates, Ltd.

Frederick W. Wackerle, Fred Wackerle, Inc.
Tom Watkins, LAI Ward Howell.
Daniel C. Weir, Daniel Wier & Associates.
William H. Willis, William Willis Worldwide, Inc.
Dale Winston, Battalia Winston International.
Ron Zingaro, Zingaro and Company.

CONCLUSION

Each of the recruiters who contributed advice and examples to this book had a distinctive set of lessons to offer to ambitious executives. But there's one reality they all agree on: success in a management position takes more than a first-class resume.

Now, more than ever, the intangibles are what will ultimately land executives in a top job. And for the recruiters who increasingly serve as the gatekeepers of Corporate America's executive suites, executive presence is the touchstone for determining management potential.

INDEX

ABOUT THE AUTHOR

A veteran of executive recruiting, Sharon Voros has helped headhunters assess executive candidates and communicate about executive presence for thousands of recruiting assignments.

Formerly vice president of communications for Ray & Berndtson, the world's sixth largest executive search firm, she has also advised recruiters at most of the world's major recruiting firms about evaluating executive presence and communicating it effectively to clients. She has conducted courses on executive assessment and search communications for the Association of Executive Search Consultants, the industry's premier trade association.

Voros's books include *Secrets from the Search Firm Files* (1997), a collaborative effort with Dr. John Rau, former dean of Indiana University's School of Business, and *Navigating Your Career* (1998). She is a regular contributor to *The National Business Employment Weekly* and *The Fordyce Letter*, and her article have been published in *The Wall Street Journal*, the *New York Times* and *The Washington Post*, *Fortune*, *CFO*, *The Harvard Business Review*, *Leaders*, *Chief Executive Officer*, *Management Review*, *Directors and Boards* and other business publications.

Voros's firm, Sharon Voros Communications, provides communications and marketing consulting to executive search, management consulting and financial services firms. Voros holds an M.B.A. degree in marketing from the Wharton School of the University of Pennsylvania and a B.A. degree cum laude from Smith College.